POWERFUL COLLEGE ADMISSION ESSAYS

POWERFUL COLLEGE ADMISSION ESSAYS

A Guide to Telling Your Story

BRENNAN BARNARD AND
SHEREEM HERNDON-BROWN

JOHNS HOPKINS UNIVERSITY PRESS
Baltimore

 Published 2025
Printed in the United States of America on acid-free paper
9 8 7 6 5 4 3 2 1

Johns Hopkins University Press
2715 North Charles Street
Baltimore, Maryland 21218
www.press.jhu.edu

Library of Congress Cataloging-in-Publication Data

Names: Barnard, Brennan, 1974– author | Herndon-Brown, Shereem, 1974– author
Title: Powerful college admission essays : a guide to telling your story / Brennan Barnard and Shereem Herndon-Brown.
Description: Baltimore : Johns Hopkins University Press, 2025. | Includes index.
Identifiers: LCCN 2025012909 | ISBN 9781421453682 paperback | ISBN 9781421453699 ebook
Subjects: LCSH: College applications | Universities and colleges—Admission | Essay—Authorship
Classification: LCC LB2351.5 .B375 2025 | DDC 808.06/6378—dc23/eng/20250515
LC record available at https://lccn.loc.gov/2025012909

A catalog record for this book is available from the British Library.

Special discounts are available for bulk purchases of this book. For more information, please contact Special Sales at specialsales@jh.edu.

EU GPSR Authorized Representative
LOGOS EUROPE, 9 rue Nicolas Poussin,
17000, La Rochelle, France
E-mail: Contact@logoseurope.eu

To the memory of our mothers, Marjorie Darling Barnard
and Leeora Arrington Brown, the strong women who
raised us and began our stories: thank you for
sharing your stories and encouraging us to write our own

Contents

Preface

Our Origin Story

Legs dangle from atop our perch on the stacked beds, nearly a dozen high school boys packed into the narrow quarters. Black, White, Colombian, Armenian, rural, urban, rich, poor, athletic, not—our backgrounds are as diverse as the conversation. It's 2:00 a.m. on a warm spring Pennsylvania morning in 1991. From girls, family, and sports to politics, religion, and college, our discussion reflects what—at that age—seemed like a complex moment in time. Soon, we are plotting the potential mischief we can engage in, and this is as much as we will share to protect the innocent. It is here our story begins.

Over three decades later, a deep friendship continues as we share careers helping young people tell their own stories. Does the paragraph above leave you wanting to know more about our backgrounds, experiences, and futures? We hope so, and this book aims to empower you to write in ways that will draw admission reviewers in when they read your college application essay. We expound on our journeys in this preface, and we want to highlight our hopes for you, applicant and loved ones, as a family—however you might define that—as you apply to college.

Our Own Stories

Brennan

I was raised on a small gentleman's farm in what was rural Pennsylvania, the middle of three boys in a Quaker family. Weekends were spent outdoors, either working around the house or on active family adventures. I was educated in a Quaker school from the start and was a "lifer" at Westtown School from kindergarten through high school graduation. My extended maternal family mostly lived locally, and the rest of the family was spread around New England—Massachusetts, Connecticut, and Maine.

Honestly, at the time, my story felt unremarkable, largely due to what I saw as my relative privilege. Though we did not have a picket fence, my nuclear family resembled what might be considered the quintessential "all-American family." For most of my life, my mother stayed at home with us while my father, an attorney who had started his own private practice, worked long hours. He was a picture of social mobility, having earned scholarships to attend some of the most selective schools in the country after growing up with limited resources. Education and family were of paramount importance, and my parents reinforced this at every step of my journey into adulthood. There was never a question of whether I would attend college.

Though I was hell-bent on going to college far from my Pennsylvania upbringing, I found myself at Franklin and Marshall College, an hour away. I studied psychology and Spanish, intrigued by people's stories and understanding them through their language and personality. The plan was to earn a doctorate in psychology and become a therapist. I took two years "off" to teach before intending to enroll in a PsyD program, but I caught the education bug and never looked back. A master's degree from the University of Vermont in higher education and student affairs confirmed my interest in the potential transformative moment between high school and college, when young people are wrestling with identity and exploring their defining stories. And here I am 30 years later, still eager to help these stories come to life.

Shereem

If you were born and raised in Brooklyn, New York, you understand that it's not a borough; it's a blood type. I carry it with me even after five decades of life because there are some things that New York City, and especially Brooklyn, taught me as a 1970s and '80s baby.

I grew up an only child attending a private Quaker school in the affluent section of Brooklyn Heights. My home, however, was in Bedford-Stuyvesant, and I was exposed daily to the stark contrast between prosperity and poverty, though we were not poor—my mom was a nurse and my dad a UPS truck driver. Growing up, I was observant and recognized life in stories. I "people watched" incessantly, gave everyone a story, and loved it. I was an avid reader of Marvel comics and got a new story about a favorite character every month. While I was an X-Men and New Mutants devotee, I enjoyed Power Pack and the Fantastic Four. Each group had a story, and each member had an even deeper story. I still remember many of them even today.

Transferring to Westtown School, another Quaker school, as a sophomore in 1989 was necessary. For me to realize the dreams that my parents had for me, I knew that I needed to be away from home. Boarding school is different from what many kids from Bed-Stuy do, but I was curious, and it was the right choice. This is where Brennan and I met and began to connect. Neither of us will say we were best friends, but there was always a mutual respect that has only grown over the last 35 years.

My story—Brooklyn to Westtown to Wesleyan University, teacher to administrator to entrepreneur—had no road map. Thus, I know it's "different." I want you, student, to see your life as awesomely different and be proud of where you're from and where you are going. One slice of your wonderfully unique life will be revealed in your personal essay for college admission.

Together

Over 35 years, we have shared experiences, struggles, successes, joys, and fears. We have held similar jobs, raised sons and daughters, and coauthored books. We have each worked in independent school admission, college admission, high school counseling, and have consulted for individuals and schools. We have joined fraternities, earned master's degrees, navigated the athletic recruiting process with children, made and lost friends, and come to terms with our mortality at our common age of 50.

We agree on many things, but there are also areas where our perspectives and approaches differ. You will see that reflected in our guidance on writing in this book. Difference is healthy and representative of storytelling. There is no right way to communicate what makes you, you. However, there are useful strategies that will allow you to highlight your unique strengths, interests, and background.

The college application is more than a form: it is an opportunity for you to communicate your story, the one only you can tell. Since each of us has a different story, each of us should have a different application and essay, and our approach to each part of this process should be, well, different.

How to Use This Book

Well begun is half done.
—Aristotle

This book is a product of our combined 50 years in the admission profession. Before we go any further, we want to make clear that not only did we both go to the same high school, Westtown School, but we also started our careers there in college counseling. Much of who we are professionally is due to our professional mentor, Susan Tree, who has been an unabashedly ethical and stalwart contributor to the college admission profession. We want to give her the well-deserved credit for where we are in our professional journeys.

Susan would put this quote from Aristotle atop the agenda every year for our college admission kickoff workshop for juniors and their families. We hope you will internalize its sentiment as you plan to tell your story for college admission, and we have structured this book to help you do just that.

You will see that the body of the book is arranged in three parts—the "Rule of Three" can be a powerful literary device and also allows us to keep this book focused. Part I is structured around *storytelling*. In chapter 1, we explore the many people who will potentially have an impact on an applicant's writing experience, including family, counselor, teachers, and, for some, friends or a mentor. Chapter 2 encourages the applicant to reflect on who they are and on their authentic voice. In chapter 3, we invite the applicant to consider the stories that have the most meaning for them and to look for unifying themes.

Part II is all about the *personal statement*, or what is widely known as the college essay. Chapter 4 outlines what it is, why colleges ask for it, and how admission offices use it. Chapter 5 discusses the types of writing prompts applicants will encounter, and we debate our different approaches to engaging with them. One of the most common questions asked about college essays is which topics to avoid. Chapter 6 addresses this issue and explores the idea of "cliché essays." Chapter 7 is about soliciting feedback and reviewing drafts to arrive at the most compelling essay possible.

Part III covers the different types of essays, supplements, short answers, and other writing asked of applicants. We explain what is being asked of the applicant and the role each type plays in admission review. Chapter 8 discusses the types of supplemental essays required for some applications, and chapter 9 digs into the "additional information" space on the application and why applicants may choose to use this opportunity or pass. In chapter 10, we explore how applicants communicate their stories beyond essays, through the activities section, emails to the admission office, and more. In chapter 11, we discuss the role of recommendations and how the voices of others contribute to the applicant's narrative. A book about writing today would not be complete without acknowledging the evolving world of artificial intelligence and the responsible use of this tool in sharing your story. So, harnessing AI is the topic of chapter 12.

We conclude with the parting question of "Is it done?" How do you know when you are ready to hit submit? What should you be thinking about as you bring your writing process to an end? We wrap the book up in as much of a bow as we can, recognizing that there is no right way to write. Let's end there. Now get typing! (or talking, as we will explain).

PART I

Storytelling

CHAPTER 1

Who Cares?

Our work is about building a community, and every community needs a variety of voices to make it dynamic. Essays give us insight into how a student thinks, what's important to them and how they might contribute to our classrooms, common rooms and other conversations across campus.

—Karen Richardson, Dean of Admission and Financial Aid, Princeton University

---

Why would we start our book with a chapter that asks, "Who cares?" Well, for one, we care, and we want you and everyone else involved in this process with you to care. (More on this below.) Although it is a bit awkward to start off this way, we want to affirm that the story you tell about a slice of your life is important. This is not something to be taken lightly or casually, but as an opportunity. Your college essay is more than a mere requirement for college applications—it's a chance to share a part of your life story and to let your personality and experiences shine. But, you might wonder, "Who really cares about my story?" The truth is that several key people care deeply about your college essay, and each for different reasons.

You Care

You care. Or you should care. If you don't, you should reevaluate whether and why you want to apply to college. Pursuing higher education is a privilege, and we want your attention to be squarely focused on your potential growth as a person and, one day, as a professional. Some of the primary reasons why we want you to take this seriously are these:

1. **College is an expensive investment in time and money.** Never waste years of your time and pay to be somewhere you do not want to be.
2. **Studies have shown that most college students do not regret the decision to attend.** While many bemoan their loan debt, most college graduates agree that the experience was worth it. It's not an easy four to six years, but over the course of life, most who did it will consider it time well spent.

Thus, we ask you, student, to care about your application writing and the stories and perspectives you are about to share because the admission process allows YOU to look inward and decide about the next phase of your educational career.

When asked to respond to a prompt or explain why you want to go to a certain school or what you can contribute there, the expectation is that you'll approach the writing with intelligent thought and a one-of-a-kind perspective. The 650-word opportunity in the personal statement or the shorter narratives of supplemental essays must show that you care about your education, school, and life. Thus, you should care about putting in maximum effort in how you brainstorm, write, implement suggestions, and proofread.

You are the most important person in this process. Your essay is a reflection of your journey, your values, and your aspirations. It's your chance to present yourself in a way no one else can.

You demonstrate your care by dedicating time and effort to crafting well-thought-out essays. This involves brainstorming, writing, revising, and proofreading. Your commitment to the process shows in the quality of your writing and the authenticity of your story. When you care about your essay, it becomes a powerful piece of writing that can move, inspire, and connect with others. It is a testament to your dedication and resilience, potentially making a significant difference in your college admission outcomes.

Why Colleges Care

Colleges care about your essay because it provides a window into who you are beyond grades and test scores. Admission officers are looking for students who will contribute to their campus community, and your essay helps them understand your character, values, and perspectives. The college application is designed to showcase more than just academic abilities; colleges seek to build diverse and dynamic communities where students excel academically, contribute to the campus culture, and embody the institution's values. The personal statement and supplemental essays play a crucial role in holistic admission review for several reasons.

Understanding You Beyond Numbers

An essay offers qualitative insight that numbers cannot capture. In your essay, you can share specific stories and experiences that illustrate your values. For instance, writing about a time when you overcame adversity or helped someone in need can demonstrate your resilience and compassion. These narratives help admission officers see the human side of your application and understand what drives you.

Grades and test scores provide a quantitative measure of a student's abilities, but they don't reveal much about the student's personality, values, and ethics

Colleges strive to create a student body with a wide range of experiences, perspectives, and talents. They aim to build a community where students from various socioeconomic backgrounds, ethnicities, and geographic locations come together to learn and grow. Your essay can highlight distinguishing aspects about your background, such as being a first-generation college student, being a legacy applicant, growing up in a multicultural household, having meaningful involvement in the community, or having lived in different countries. These experiences have shaped your worldview and provide a distinctive voice that can enrich the campus environment.

Your interests and experiences make you unique. Whether it's being part of cultural traditions, standing up for social issues, or having a hobby like taking pictures of stars, all these things have shaped who you are. Colleges want to know how these experiences will add new ideas in class and help others think differently.

Outside class, these experiences can help you with teamwork and getting involved on campus. If you've taken part in community projects, you've likely learned how to lead and work with others, which is useful in college. Your background might even inspire new clubs, events, or projects that bring students together. Whether it's starting a new group, leading a sustainability project, or planning events that celebrate different cultures, your perspective can make the campus more interesting, vibrant, and connected.

As educators who have each spent over 25 years working in college admission, we have seen firsthand how these kinds of stories can set an applicant apart. When you share personal experiences of yours, they not only show what you've accomplished, but they also give insight into your character, your problem-solving skills, and your potential to enrich a college campus.

Admission officers look for students who won't just participate in activities but who will also take initiative and bring new ideas to the table. Your essay is the perfect place to share your journey, the lessons you've learned, and how you plan to contribute to the college community. By presenting your story honestly and thoughtfully, you give the admission committee a clear view of your leadership, resilience, and the unique qualities you will bring to their school. Over the years, we've read many essays that do just that, and those essays always stand out.

By sharing your story in this way, you allow the reader to see your true self and understand how your experiences have prepared you to take on new challenges and opportunities in college. This kind of personal storytelling, rooted in real experiences and genuine reflections, has a lasting impact and truly shows the admission committee who you are beyond your grades and test scores.

Let us tell you about Emily, a high school senior whose story still stands out to me (Shereem). From a small town in the South, she noticed something that most others had ignored—the town's park had fallen into disrepair. Overgrown grass, trash everywhere, and a pond that hadn't been cleaned in ages. What made Emily different was that she didn't just shrug it off. She decided to do something about it.

Instead of just attending her environmental club meetings, Emily took the lead in organizing a full-scale cleanup of the park. She gathered her classmates, reached out to local businesses for donations, and even coordinated with the town council to get the necessary permissions. It wasn't easy. She faced pushback from some people in the community who were skeptical of her plans, and on the day of the cleanup, bad weather almost derailed everything. But Emily didn't back down. She pushed through every obstacle and made the project happen.

In her essay, Emily didn't just focus on the result—though the park was transformed with clean pathways, freshly planted flowers, and a restored playground. She shared the entire process: the struggles, the moments of doubt, and the lessons she learned along the way. What struck me most was her reflection on how the project didn't just improve the park; it brought the community together as well. People who had never spoken to each other before were suddenly working side by side, united in their efforts to make their town a better place.

Emily stood out because of the way she told her story. It wasn't just about what she did; it was about why she did it, what it meant to her, and how it changed her. That level of personal reflection and leadership is exactly what colleges are looking for.

She applied to several small, selective liberal arts colleges, places that value community involvement and leadership. Her essay resonated deeply with them. Two of the schools even went beyond the standard acceptance letter. They sent her personalized notes, mentioning her park project and how they could see her making a similar impact on their campus. One school awarded her a leadership scholarship because it was so impressed by her initiative and dedication.

What I remember most about Emily's application wasn't just the project she led—it was the way she made her experience come to life in her writing. She showed her passion, her grit, and her ability to bring people together. That's the kind of story that makes a real difference in admission review, and it's a perfect example of how sharing your own story can have a lasting impact.

Mission and Vision

Each college has its own mission and set of core values. In the admission process, colleges lean on these and approach their holistic evaluation with clear and actionable "institutional priorities" every year. These evolve over time, while staying rooted in what the school believes; institutional priorities can affect admission decisions and how essays are read. Your essays allow you to show how your values align with the institution's. For example, if a college emphasizes social justice, an essay about your involvement in advocacy, familial responsibilities, or volunteer work can illustrate your commitment to that ideal.

Why Parents Care

Your parents care deeply about your college essay because they want to see you succeed and achieve your dreams. They have invested in your education and well-being, and your essay is a culmination of years of hard work and support. This level of care and concern is particularly poignant in the context of today's increasingly competitive and often bewildering college admission landscape. With more students applying for a limited number of spots at selective institutions, the pressure to stand out is greater than ever. It can be overwhelming for both students and their parents, especially when procedures and standards frequently change. Together, you must navigate a maze of application requirements, deadlines, standardized tests, and financial aid forms.

Many parents are confused and concerned about how to best support their children through this process. Now, please hand this book over to your parents so we can speak to them directly.

To Parents

Parents, you're awesome for simply buying this book and wanting to support your kids the way you do. Your efforts are not going unnoticed. During the essay writing process, the best thing you can do for your child is to help them organize their thoughts and time. While encouragement is good and necessary, sitting down with them and caring enough to brainstorm ideas and discuss timelines and deadlines for the writing process, ideally over the summer before their senior year, will lead to a much happier home and a smoother fall. Dedicating an hour a week when you can all sit down together and review the elements of the process, especially the state of the writing, is fair and necessary. We do not encourage parents to direct their kids to undertake writing alone; college is an expensive investment, and your teenager is likely unsure of what to do and where to go, and thus needs to lean into you.

More parental responsibility? Yes, and you're built for it. You know your teen better than they know themselves, and though it may have been a while since you were in college, if ever at all, today is a new day and everyone needs to see what is happening in college admission and how they can help. Your job, tangibly, beyond encouragement and assisting with goal-setting is best done at the bookends of the process: brainstorming and proofreading.

There are four key stages of the essay writing process—brainstorming, writing, implementing suggestions for revision, and proofreading. You can be of most help during brainstorming and proofreading. Obviously, you shouldn't write essays for your teen, and the feedback you offer may not be received well since you probably are not a school counselor or admission officer. Of course you can have an opinion, and depending on your relationship with your child, maybe you share it. At minimum, please proofread the essay for "final" approval and resist the urge to polish it with your own language and writing style. No, this is not your essay, nor is it fair or ethical for your fingerprints to be on it.

We get it, though. As a parent, we want the best for our kids, especially when it comes to something as important (and stressful) as college admission. We've been there, both as parents and as educators, and we know how overwhelming it can feel. Take it from us—this process can either bring you closer to your child or make everyone in the house a little crazy. But with the right approach, you can help your child without adding to the pressure. Let us share another story that might help.

A few years ago, I (Shereem) worked with a family whose son, Alex, was a high school senior with big dreams of getting into a top-tier college. His parents were right there with him, feeling all the stress and uncertainty. Like most parents, they knew the importance of his college essay but weren't sure how to support him without taking over. They were stuck between wanting to help and not knowing exactly how to do it.

If this sounds familiar, don't worry—you're not alone. Alex's parents took the right approach, and we think doing the same may make all the difference for you, too.

Alex's parents knew that constantly asking, "How's the essay going?" wasn't going to help. We love our kids, but let's be real—sometimes we can smother them without realizing it. Instead, Alex's parents chose one day a week to check in on his progress and left it at that. The rest of the time, they focused on creating a calm, supportive environment. No nagging, no extra pressure—just space. And you know what? It worked. Alex felt less stressed, and his parents were able to support him without adding to his anxiety.

Get Feedback from the Right People

Even as parents, we can't be experts in everything, and that's okay. Alex's parents recognized this and signed him up for a college essay workshop. There, he got feedback from people who know what admission officers look for. It wasn't about taking over the process but rather helping him improve his writing with some outside perspectives. If you can find similar workshops or resources, we highly recommend it. Sometimes, hearing advice from someone who isn't Mom or Dad can make all the difference.

Sometimes, despite our best efforts, we just need an expert. That's where I came in. Alex's parents hired me to work with their son on his essay. They spent time brainstorming, revising, and digging deep to help him tell his story in a way that was true to who he is. He wrote about his time volunteering at an animal shelter—not just listing what he did but explaining how it shaped him into someone who values responsibility and compassion. By the end, his essay wasn't just another requirement—it was a reflection of his growth.

Parents, we don't have to be the experts, but we can be the support system our kids need. Alex's parents knew when to step back, when to get feedback, and when to bring in help. Their guidance helped him craft an essay that truly represented him—and ultimately, that's what colleges want to see.

While college admission can be an exciting time for family bonding and creating memories, it can also be complicated and layered with challenges. This is especially true with writing.

Family, however you define yours, can play a significant role in the college admission experience. We believe this so fervently that we both wrote previous books focused on the importance of family relationships and dynamics when searching for, applying to, and affording college.

Most of a college application feels largely predetermined because it asks for an account of the past: classes taken, grades earned, activities done. Essays, on the other hand, remain a factor not yet determined that can influence the outcome of an admission decision. Because we are both parents, we know how prone we and other parents are to try and control outcomes, and it can be difficult to loosen our grip. Now is the time, and with some thoughtful planning, it CAN be done.

Many parents are used to assisting their children with homework, proofreading English and history papers and weighing in with opinions on content and grammar. As a middle and high school student I (Brennan) had countless battles with my parents over papers that I felt were "good enough." Often these moments ended with tears and essays soiled in red pen. Admittedly (don't tell them) it made me a better writer, but the road to that place was bumpy.

Here are some facts:

- Parents with writing-intensive jobs have a lot of practice.
- College-educated parents have likely written a lot of papers.

- Age sometimes brings wisdom.
- Parents usually know their children best.

Here are some more facts:

- A legal brief, patient summary, insurance claim, or some other job-related document is very different from a college essay.
- If a parent applied to college themselves, it has probably been a while.
- Age doesn't always equal wisdom.
- Children sometimes know themselves best.

Ultimately the college essay belongs to the applicant and should be their prerogative. If students feel a lack of ownership, it is easy for them to disengage with this important part of the application. When parents dominate the process, their child tends to detach, which creates a frustrating cycle and lack of progress. Voice in writing matters, and it is clear to readers when an essay sounds more parent than child.

Set Expectations

Make a contract as a family about the essay: when it will be written and what role each person will play. The student should take the lead here and outline the support they would like from their parents. It could be that the student doesn't want their parents to have any hand in this, and that should be honored. It is called the "personal statement" for a reason. We have worked with many students who wrote about an issue that they preferred their family not read about. Though that can be hard to accept, we parents must. For these students, it helps when parents can agree with this and the student can agree to let someone else, maybe a counselor or teacher, support them by reviewing their writing.

For those students who are willing to have family play a role, below are some areas where family can become involved. Decide together ahead of time what that involvement will be, so there is no misunderstanding down the road about what you agreed on. In fact, we recommend *putting it in writing* how the family has agreed to take part in the writing process.

Brainstorming Topics

How much input does the applicant want on what to write about, and when do they want input? Some parents have an essay topic in mind that they are convinced would make their student stand out. We recommend some tongue-biting here and allowing the student to surface ideas first. Decide if and when parents might suggest possible topics.

Reviewing and Proofreading

We will elaborate on how best to seek feedback in chapter 7. For now, agree on whether parents will give feedback and how much.

- Does the student want input on grammar or on content, that is, whether the essay captures the essence of what they are trying to communicate?
- Will proofreading be a one-time event or a repeated process?
- Will the student ask other reviewers to give input, and if so, who?

Work out the answers now so that all are assured of having made a plan.

Timeline

Having a timeline is perhaps the most important thing to put in writing. Work together to set a schedule for completing the application essays. Work backwards from the application due date and set check-in points so that the writing process doesn't become a constant conversation or source of tension. Maybe you decide to have a final draft a month before the first application's deadline, so put dates on the calendar when you will have a rough draft, seek input, revise, and proofread.

Don't Be This Dad

Years ago, I (Brennan) worked with a family who let down their guard in establishing boundaries in the admission experience. The son, call him Charlie, was a responsible student and applicant who conducted a thoughtful search of schools, met deadlines, and drafted a thorough application. His father, call him John, had faith in his son and had been supportive from the outset, allowing Charlie to take the lead. When it came to application submission, however, John insisted on having final say, requiring that he review the application himself and hit submit. After all, he argued, it was his credit card that would pay the application fee. Charlie capitulated, and the application was submitted by John to the five schools to which Charlie was applying for early admission.

Weeks later, Charlie looked over his application after being denied by the first school. He was wondering if he should change anything when applying to the remaining schools on his list. That is when he noticed the surprise. There was a sentence in his personal statement that he did not write himself. You guessed it . . . John had taken liberties in his pre-submission review, adding a few thoughts he believed would strengthen the essay. Here is the kicker: he had misspelled a word. Furthermore, the sentence didn't enhance the content or character of the writing.

Was this the reason Charlie was denied? Of course not. He received a number of acceptances to schools that were great matches, has since graduated from college, and is thriving as a young professional. But his applying to college didn't need to go this way, and this blunder created anxiety for Charlie and strained the trust between father and son. Totally avoidable.

An Opportunity

We recommend that you approach the writing process as a family and use it as an opportunity to come together and have a shared experience rather than turning it into a task that hangs over your heads and creates rifts. Having dedicated conversations and clear expectations at the outset will put you on the road to essay success and family harmony.

CHAPTER 2

Ethics, Authenticity, and You

The personal essay provides insights into the person—the human—we are reading about and is an opportunity for the student to share something that matters to them in their own voice. It's a chapter, so to speak, in the student's life. A moment in time.

—Claudia Marroquin, Senior Vice President and Dean of Admissions and Student Aid, Bowdoin College

---

What does it mean to write an ethical essay? At a foundational level, an essay needs to be your work, be truthful, and ideally reveal the strength of your character (something colleges care a lot about). If you are reading this book and putting in the work, then hopefully you are already dedicated to owning this experience and doing so ethically. In the age of artificial intelligence (discussed in chapter 12), it can be tempting to allow ChatGPT or other emerging technology tools to take over your process. Don't. As with every aspect of your college application, the essay is about establishing a relationship with the reader. If there is any doubt whether your representation of who you are and what you've done is honest and accurate, then your candidacy is in jeopardy.

Keep in mind that seasoned admission professionals have read thousands of essays and can quickly identify when an applicant's writing is not their own. If the essay either does not match the rest of the application's tone and content or sounds like the voice of another, you plant seeds of doubt. This book is about finding your voice and then honoring it, so stay the course.

What does it mean to "keep it real" in college admission? *Authenticity* is one of those buzzwords in admission that gets used so often that it starts to lose meaning (see also *passion* and *holistic*). What does it mean to share one's authentic voice? As mentioned already, at the most basic level, it requires an ethical approach to writing that guarantees an essay or other submission is in fact the applicant's own work. But authenticity takes it a step further by being *true to who you are*. You can write an ethical essay that tries too hard to be something you're not and is, therefore, inauthentic.

In the admission process, which seems judgmental and demanding, it is natural that you would try to tell colleges what you think they want to hear. By doing this, though, you only end up losing your uniqueness and the qualities that have the potential to make you stand out. Said plainly, if you have to *try* to be authentic, then you're inherently not being so.

Consider these reflections on authenticity from college admission leaders:

> *Being your authentic self should come naturally and easily. We want you to be "you" because as much as you want to be here at our university, it's important that the "you" who shows up is comfortable and doesn't sacrifice their own needs to fulfill some perception that "this school" wants "this version of you" and this is how you will achieve enlightenment and the path to contentment.*
>
> —Jody Glassman, Assistant Vice President of Enrollment and University Admissions, Florida International University

> *Conveying authenticity is difficult because it contradicts applicants' overall need to spotlight their achievements and plans.*

Our authentic selves (at age 17 or 50) have limits, uncertainties, and gaps. I find these emerge best in essays, not as a deliberate ploy to demonstrate authenticity, but when students accept the least amount of help from well-meaning adults itching to edit their work. Some applicants' entire personal statements can be somewhat meandering, pointless, and unhelpful in ways that no adult reader would have allowed—and thereby scream "authenticity" that can help the rest of the application click.

—Jonathan Burdick, former Vice Provost for Enrollment, Cornell University

Authenticity may be a lost art form for a generation of applicants exposed to reality TV and social media "likes." My one piece of advice? Step away from social media apps for a quiet hour of reflection then call a friend or family member and have a real conversation in real-time. It may be awkward at first, but it will better prepare you to finish that college essay, better engage in the classroom this term, and be more comfortable talking with a future roommate.

—Catherine McDonald Davenport, former Vice President for Enrollment and Dean of Admissions, Dickinson College

A great way to check for authenticity is to simply read your application aloud to yourself. If it sounds like you, then what you're sharing and presenting is authentic. If you question some elements of your application or trip up on phrases while reading it aloud, then chances are you've strayed a bit from your authentic self. You can fix that by going back and reworking certain portions of your application to feel confident that all is coming from your voice.

—Leigh A. Weisenburger, Vice President for Enrollment and Dean of Admission and Financial Aid, Bates College

Even if the materials in the application don't show all of you, they can still work to authentically represent you. If each of the things you share in your application is actually something you care about, and you tell us about it in the way you communicate in your day-to-day life, then those details can represent you well.

—Whitney Soule, Vice Provost and Dean of Admissions, University of Pennsylvania

This idea of being "authentic" tends to come up with essays. What do I write about? How do I "stand out"? I've always found that the best essays are the ones that showcase a student's authentic self. It doesn't have to be about a life-changing event, but rather a normal day in life or honestly just a short moment in time that conveys who a student is; those are the essays I like to read. My first dean of admission, when I was a first-year admission counselor over 20 years ago said this about what made a good essay: "if I were to pick up your essay off the ground and had no idea what application it was connected to and read it, then, by the end, had a really good sense of who you are." That's always stuck with me. Who you are, not who you think we want you to be; just who you are.

—Eric Nichols, Vice President for Enrollment Management, Loyola University Maryland

Authenticity happens when your representation of yourself is consistent with facts about you, your thoughts, and what you do.

—Gil J. Villanueva, Vice President for Enrollment, Rhodes College

Applicants should present themselves in their fullest and truest sense. Admission offices want to learn about the individual and their particularity and peculiarity: their strengths, the ways in

which they are perfectly flawed, and what makes them "tick," no matter what that is.

—Jay Jacobs, Vice Provost for Enrollment Management, University of Vermont

Having read many, many applications and essays over the last 25 years, I have found it truly is the case that if a student writes about an event, person, experience, or topic that is meaningful to them, that sought after authenticity will be evident. When you write about something you truly care about, were impacted by, or that was particularly influential, the reader can feel the impact the individual experienced, often in a tangible way. The old adage "write what you know" certainly applies to the college admission essay. Colleges look to the essay often as one of the few ways we can learn more about who the student is and what sort of community member they might be, and that is best determined (and most authentic) when the topic is meaningful to the student.

—Stefanie D. Niles, President, Cottey College

Students are authentic if they use their best voice but do not overwrite with excessive dramatic flair. Students are authentic when they actually tell us what their motivations are for their activities and success in high school and their goals as they have so far formed them for college majors and career interests. If the student's essays and comments on their activities and goals seem to match up with the teacher and counselor recommendations on them, we are more confident we are seeing the actual person emerging in the review.

—Don Bishop, former Associate Vice President for Undergraduate Enrollment, University of Notre Dame

When I was a kid, my mother's most constant refrain was "it's not what you say, but how you say it" that matters. And while

she was usually referring to how I spoke to my brothers, the truth is more universal. Introducing yourself authentically to a college is as much about your voice, how you articulate yourself, as it is what you talk about. It's your voice, your personality that we are interested in reading and hearing. Being authentic means being truthful about who you are and what matters to you.

—Sally Stone Richmond, Vice President for Admissions and Financial Aid, Washington and Lee University

As you dig further into this book and learn approaches to writing for college applications, keep your ethical compass pointing due north and stay true to yourself, and the rest will fall into place.

Eulogy Not Resume

Stay with us here: one of the hardest things for any of us to consider is dying. This is especially true in one's teens. We don't mean to offer doom and gloom; instead, we want you to understand that when it comes to your personal essay, it may help to see it as a *eulogy*. And what does that mean? The essay gives you an opportunity to share with others the important experiences or learning that you are doing during your young life. It starts with what's important to you, who is important to you, what you have learned from experience, and how you have applied it.

The personal essay is all about your heart. It's about how you feel about yourself, how you feel about others, and what your heart is going to give. As corny or cheesy as that may sound, colleges are looking for students who want to be givers. Personal essays are more reflective than they are aspirational. While there may be a hint of what you hope to do in the future, you must lean into lived experience:

- What is important to you?
- How has your experience brought you to this point?

- Who are you becoming?
- How is your experience fueling your life ambitions?

In his book *The Road to Character*, author David Brooks introduces the idea of *resume virtues*, one's skills and achievements, and *eulogy virtues*, the values that indicate a "life well lived." This is a great framework for the college essay—it is a eulogy, not a resume. Focus on the following.

Character over achievements. While a resume highlights your achievements, skills, and qualifications, a eulogy celebrates who you are as a person—your virtues, impact on others, and the values you embody. For college essays, this means focusing on your personal growth, integrity, compassion, and the lessons learned from your experiences.

Authenticity and depth. Admission officers want to understand who you are beyond your grades and extracurricular activities. Write in a way that reflects your true self. Share stories that reveal your passions, challenges, and the moments that have shaped your worldview.

Impact and legacy. Consider how you want to be remembered and the legacy you wish to leave. Write about the ways you've made a positive impact on friends, your community, or a cause. This demonstrates not only your values but also your potential to contribute meaningfully to the college community.

Virtuous qualities. Highlight qualities such as empathy, resilience, humility, and generosity. Instead of boasting about accolades, illustrate how these qualities have manifested in your life. For example, instead of merely stating you were the captain of the soccer team, describe how you led with kindness and encouraged teamwork. This kind of vulnerability is respected, so please don't be afraid to show it. This can make your essay more relatable and impactful.

Avoid overt bragging. Humility is a key component of virtuous writing. Even when discussing your accomplishments, frame them in a way that highlights teamwork, gratitude, and the support of others. Be proud of who you are, not arrogant about what you have done.

The following example contrasts the two approaches:

Resume Approach

"I was the president of the student council, captain of the debate team, and volunteered 200 hours at the local homeless shelter."

Eulogy Approach

"As president of the student council, I learned the importance of listening to diverse perspectives and building consensus. Leading the debate team taught me the value of perseverance and respect for opposing views. My time volunteering at the local homeless shelter was humbling; it reminded me daily of the strength and dignity found in every person, regardless of their circumstances."

Head vs. Heart in College Essays

A statement I (Shereem) often use with students is this: *Personal essays come from the heart, and supplemental essays are from the head.* In parts II and III of this book, we explore these distinctions in more depth, but here is a primer.

Supplemental Essays

Supplemental essays, often required by colleges in addition to the main personal statement, are designed to gauge your intellectual engagement, understanding of the institution, and specific motivations for applying. These essays should be crafted with clarity, logic, and detailed knowledge about the school and its offerings. Here's why they need to come from your *head*.

Focus on fit. Supplemental essays often ask why you want to attend that particular school or why you are interested in a specific program. To answer effectively, you must research the school's distinguishing features, academic programs, extracurricular opportunities, and values. This requires intellectual effort and strategic thinking.

Analytical approach. These essays demand a clear, logical structure. Admission officers are looking for evidence that you can think critically and articulate your thoughts coherently. Whether it's explaining how a program aligns with your career goals or discussing a book that influenced your perspective, your responses should be well organized and demonstrate analytical depth.

Showcase your knowledge. Schools want to see that you have a genuine interest in them and that you've done your homework. Mentioning specific courses, professors, research opportunities, or the campus culture shows that you've thoughtfully considered why this institution is the right fit for you. While these essays should be structured and research-driven, showing enthusiasm and personal connection to the school can enhance your writing.

Personal Essays

On the other hand, personal essays, such as the Common Application personal statement, are your opportunity to showcase your personality, values, and experiences. These essays should be heartfelt and genuine, reflecting your inner self. Here's why they need to come from your *heart*.

Emotional connection. The best personal essays evoke emotion. Whether it's a moment of triumph, a significant challenge, or a life-changing experience, your essay should make the reader feel something. This emotional connection is what makes your essay memorable and helps you stand out in a sea of applicants.

Reflective depth. Writing from the heart requires introspection. It's about reflecting on your life experiences and considering how they have influenced your growth and aspirations. This depth of reflection demonstrates maturity and self-awareness, qualities that colleges value in prospective students.

Writing about who you are, what is important to you, and who you are becoming are essential to approaching college application writing. Win or lose—meaning being admitted or not—the personal essay is about what you believe. Write proudly and confidently.

CHAPTER 3

The Power of Stories

College applications capture the "what" of an applicant in relatively simple fashion. The most compelling candidates, however, find ways to spotlight their "how" and "why." Stories bring action and explorations (the how) to life and elevate motivations (the why) in a beautifully informative fashion. A storified personal statement often energizes an application and allows the reader a deeper awareness of candidate character and presence.

—Matthew Hyde, Dean of Admissions and Financial Aid, Trinity College

"Kuplink, kuplank, kaplunk!" Robert McCloskey's *Blueberries for Sal* is a story that is still etched in my (Brennan's) mind over 40 years after I first heard it. It is an adventure steeped in family, natural abundance, and curiosity, which is maybe why it continues to resonate with me. Or perhaps my love of these things—and blueberries—are born out of hearing the story over and over. After all, "the ripest berries were always a little further along the path."

What Is a Story?

In their purest form, stories are a tool of communication. They are a way of sharing the past, a series of experiences, or, in some cases, imagined scenarios. In college admission, an applicant's story serves as a snapshot of their life and an opportunity to stand out among other qualified students. To be an effective storyteller, you need to match your style of writing with what the audience is asking for.

When you read or listen to stories, what are you drawn to? Are there common genres, topics, or themes in what you read? What tales and books do you remember from your childhood? However you digest stories—watch movies or shows, go to a library or bookstore, or search on Audible or Amazon—what are you looking for?

Spend some time reflecting on the types of stories that make you laugh, cry, become curious, or encourage you. Why do they resonate, and what aspects become lasting memories?

What NOT to Do

"Pattern matching" is one of the greatest mistakes that students can make in college admission. Don't try to replicate what a previous applicant did who was admitted to your dream school. For example, say there were two applicants from your high school who were accepted at MIT in the past five years. Both were president of the Robotics Club, spent their summer interning at a local tech firm, and tutored other students taking in Multivariable Calculus. It is tempting to assume that your chances of being admitted will likewise increase if you follow this same formula. Incorrect.

The essay is one area where pattern matching emerges most prominently. An applicant might have been admitted to Brown University after writing a compelling essay about their family dinners, reflecting on the diversity of their ethnic cuisine. However, this topic and their admission do not share a causal relationship, nor is writing a similar essay a strategic approach to your acceptance. Do yourself a favor and don't rush out to buy a book called *College Essays That Worked.* Don't fixate on essay examples from previous applicants. In other words, read and listen to more stories and pay less attention to others' college essays.

Make a List

Okay, back to the question with which we began this chapter: What stories are you drawn to? If you do not regularly read or listen to stories, now might be a good time to begin. Start a story reading list or podcast queue and see what stands out. Ask teachers, friends, and family for their recommendations of where to find good stories. While you're at it, have them explain why they especially like the stories they are suggesting. Take this opportunity to read a memoir by a favorite celebrity, historical figure, or creative writer. In many ways, the college essay is like a mini-memoir.

Two places you might begin are the podcasts *The Moth Radio Hour* and *This I Believe*. Both are outlets for storytelling, and the stories you will hear are personal and honest and make the teller vulnerable.

Check It Twice

Now that you have a list, dig in and take note. What are the common themes that speak to you in the stories that stand out? You might have to go back and read or listen to a story more than once.

- Are there ways of starting stories that instantly make you want to learn more?
- Are there approaches to final sentences that leave you with a lasting impression?
- What doesn't work for you?
- Do you find your attention drifting when the story lacks imagery or becomes redundant?

Be curious and listen or read with the mind of a researcher.

What Is Your Story Worth?

You might have heard of the company Storyworth. It offers a gift subscription meant to "preserve meaningful moments and memories in a beautiful keepsake book." With a subscription, a friend or family member of the subscriber is sent a brief writing prompt each week for a year, and then Storyworth curates their responses into a cohesive story that can be shared.

Here are some example prompts from the website:

- What things matter most to you in life?
- What things did your parents argue about when you were little?
- Which family members do you wish you kept better in touch with?
- What are some of your fondest holiday memories?
- What are your favorite possessions? Why?
- What things are you proudest of in your life?
- Who was one of your first crushes? What was special about them?
- What is one of the strangest things that has ever happened to you?
- How is life different today compared to when you were a child?

Try this with some friends or family for a few weeks and see what emerges: Take turns coming up with essay questions/prompts. Each of you then takes 15–20 minutes to respond to the prompt with freewriting. Think of it as an extended Snapchat exchange.

A Proud Father

Of the thousands of college essays that I (Brennan) have reviewed as an admission officer and counselor, one that stands out as a favorite was written by my son Sam (and I am not even biased!). I was very hands-off when my kids applied to college. After two decades in the profession of college counseling, I know enough to be dangerous and have seen the admission experience create rifts between young people and their parents. I was so cautionary that my son finally asked me in September of his senior year if I was going to ask to see his essay or not. I told him that it was his prerogative and I was willing to but not assuming to.

Later that day, Sam's essay was in my email inbox. Minutes later, my eyes were welling with tears, my heart was full, and any concerns I had about his candidacy for admission were allayed. I bring up his essay because it was, in fact, about storytelling. He brought to life a moment with his grandfather (my dad) when they examined a family relic, a rifle from the Revolutionary War. From a family of Quakers and pacifists, Sam reflected on the meaning of the object, but the larger message was about the legacy of family stories and how he shares his appreciation of this telling of history with his grandfather.

The Chapters of Your Life

Writing is a process, and whether you are drafting a lab report, analytical essay, or memoir, it can be helpful to make an outline before jumping in. Telling your authentic story in college admission is no different. Ultimately, colleges will read your application as a series of chapters. So it is useful for you to think about your life experiences in the same way and to make sure you are telling the whole story.

Take some time to reflect on memories and brainstorm with your family and friends to identify different phases or aspects of your life. How would you categorize the different parts of you? For some it might be chronological—a timeline of events and experiences. Others might dedicate their chapters to different interests. There is no right way. The point is that it is useful to step back and take account of your life so far. What stands out as notable or distinguishing in your journey?

Here is how a chapter outline might look:

Chapter 1. Childhood

Chapter 2. Family

Chapter 3. Community and Context

Chapter 4. Interests and Involvement

Chapter 5. School and Academics

Chapter 6. Unique Experiences

Chapter 7. Special Relationships

Chapter 8. Strengths and Accomplishments

Chapter 9. Who Are You Becoming?

Next, make a brief outline for each chapter with bullet points about memories, moments, people, or places. Don't overthink this; just jot down whatever comes to mind. You are now equipped with a wealth of prompts from which you can choose. Don't try to draft a full essay; just write a few vignettes, or brief stories, that relate to these different chapters, experiences, and memories. A topic will emerge and speak to you, but first, you must fill your bucket with ideas. "Kuplink, kuplank, kaplunk!"

PART II

Personal Statement

CHAPTER 4

The Personal Statement

The personal essay is valuable because it is so . . . personal. Evaluators aren't looking for the "right" answer, we're looking for your real answer—in the way you would normally write and describe your thoughts. Not a stream of consciousness, but also not a mashup of input and edits from lots of other people. If too many others influence your writing, it becomes a "people" essay, not a "personal" essay, and we lose the plot on you.

—Whitney Soule, Vice Provost and Dean of Admissions, University of Pennsylvania

---

The personal statement is what most people understand to be "the college essay." While students may already believe—or hear it said—that it is the most important piece of writing in a college application, that is not always the case. Is it important? Yes. However, given the many components of the college application, we want to remind students, parents, and educators that application review begins and oftentimes ends with the transcript. College admission officers may not read any of an applicant's essays if their four-year history of grades is not competitive for the application pool.

Now that we've gotten that out of the way, let's discuss what the personal statement is. Consider the words *personal* and *statement*. Understandably, students want to, and need to, make a statement about who they are, what's important to them, who they are becoming, and who they aspire to be. Bravo! Now, imagine being an admission officer at a college and wanting to make the best-informed decisions for the college's entering first-year class but having to read hundreds, if not thousands, of these statements. Because teenagers often have similar life experiences, many of these essays will sound alike. There are similar themes of failure, loss, adversity, perseverance, and declarations of "what I will be when I grow up." Admirable, yes, but original, no.

We are not trying to be mean here. Still, we are trying to be direct: students must use their personal essay to tell colleges a story about growth, intellectual maturity, or something celebratory about themselves. Given their life experiences or academic pursuits, students must take the approach that attending college and even writing this essay is an opportunity and a privilege. The personal statement is the non-numerical core of your college application. It is a moment to step outside a formulaic approach to getting in and to make your case for admission in a meaningful and personal way.

A personal essay allows students to showcase their individuality, personality, and experiences beyond their academic record and test scores. It allows them to highlight their unique qualities, passions, and perspectives, offering a glimpse into their character. We encourage students to "document, don't create," which allows them to be introspective, possibly vulnerable, and introduce themselves. When you "document" what has happened in your life, you share, show, and reveal. When you try to "create," the essay can sometimes become abstract and vague. The person who is reading it does not know you and may not get a chance to meet you in person. You have minutes, if not seconds, to capture the reader's attention. Hence, this is why a powerful or clever introductory sentence always has a chance of "reeling in the reader." Yes, the essay must develop over the next several paragraphs, but the introduction is key.

What Do We Mean by Documenting?

Simply put, documenting means reflecting on the moments that have shaped you, the experiences that have taught you something, or the relationships that have impacted who you are. Your story is already inside you. Your job is to uncover it, not invent it.

The personal statement can have a significant influence in selective college admission, where thousands of applicants have similar grade point averages, test scores, and impressive extracurriculars. So the critical question is, **What do they actually want to learn from your personal essay?**

Most colleges aren't just looking for academically strong students; they're seeking individuals who will contribute to their campus community with their curiosity, self-awareness, and growth. They want to admit students who can reflect on their experiences meaningfully and articulate not just *what* they've done but *why* it matters to them.

Here are some things selective colleges want to see in your essay.

Self-awareness and reflection. Admission officers want to know that you can reflect deeply. They're less interested in what you've accomplished and more intrigued by how your experiences have shaped your understanding of yourself and the world around you. What did you learn from your challenges? How have your values and interests evolved over time? How are you continuing to grow?

Authenticity. Admission officers are looking for the real you. Not the version of you that you think they want to see, but your true self. Authenticity (see chapter 2) comes across when you're honest about your experiences, vulnerabilities, and personal growth. Colleges can spot a fabricated story from a mile away, so resist the urge to "sound impressive." Instead, focus on being sincere.

Intellectual curiosity. Colleges want students who are excited about learning—not just for the sake of good grades but also because they have a genuine passion for discovery. When writing about an interest, challenge, or moment of growth, show how it has sparked your curiosity or inspired you to dig deeper into a subject.

Contribution to community. Beyond your individual experiences, colleges want to know how you interact with and contribute to your community. Have you lifted up others? Have you been open to new ideas and perspectives? For your essay, think about how your personal growth aligns with what you can contribute to the college environment.

Resilience and growth. Admission officers understand that life isn't always smooth sailing. They value essays that show you've faced challenges and come out stronger or more self-aware. How did you handle failure? What did you learn about yourself during tough times? If you have not faced significant adversity, don't feel compelled to manufacture it, but if you have, don't avoid addressing it.

Finding Pride in Your Story

It's easy to get caught up in the pressure to write the "perfect" essay, especially when you know it will be read by people who are influencing your future. But here's the truth: your essay doesn't have to be perfect (nor will it be). It just has to be *you*.

No matter what happens with admission, you should be proud of the essay you write. Why? Crafting an authentic essay that reflects your experiences, challenges, values, and growth is a significant achievement. Regardless of whether you get into your top-choice school, you've taken the time to reflect deeply on who you are, what you care about, and how you've evolved. That's a meaningful process that goes beyond college applications.

We want students to be proud of their stories and how those stories are shared. Here are a few things to remember regardless of acceptance.

You've told your story. If you've written an essay that feels true to your voice and experiences, you've already won. Many students struggle with authenticity because they're too focused on what they think admission officers want to hear. But when you write something that genuinely feels *you*, that's a victory in itself.

You've grown through reflection. Writing an essay that digs deep into who you are and what you've learned is an act of self-reflection that will serve you well. Whether or not you get into your dream school, this kind of introspection helps you grow. It's a skill that will benefit you long after the admission process.

You've shown courage. Writing about personal challenges, growth, or even passions can make you vulnerable. It takes courage to open up and share pieces of yourself with others, especially knowing how competitive college admission can be. The fact that you've done that shows bravery and maturity.

The right school for you will appreciate the real you. Writing an authentic essay might not guarantee acceptance to every school on your list, but it will ensure that the schools that do accept you are choosing you for who you truly are, not for the persona you think they want. Admission decisions, particularly at selective schools, often come down to factors beyond your control. But what you *can* control is the quality of your reflection, the honesty of your story, and the pride you take in your work. Don't judge the success of your essay solely on the outcome of your applications. Instead, recognize the value in telling a story that's true to you, regardless of where you end up.

Our Own Personal Essays

Shereem

In my personal essay, written during a pivotal time in my life, I poured out a narrative that came from the depths of my heart. I centered my story on the profound influence Darrick Hamilton had on my journey—how he guided me through the critical years when I was not just a student and an athlete but a young person striving to understand my place in the world.

My essay wasn't simply a recounting of achievements or challenges; it was an exploration of how Darrick's mentorship shaped my understanding of success, community, and self-worth. His belief in my potential pushed me to excel in areas of my life, but he also taught me that true success is deeply rooted in the relationships we build and the people we uplift along the way.

More than anything, my essay was a tribute to how he helped me align my aspirations with my core values. This realization wasn't merely an intellectual awakening; it was a deeply emotional one that shaped how I approached my studies and future aspirations.

Today, Dr. Darrick Hamilton is the Henry Cohen Professor of Economics and Urban Policy and the founding Director of the Institute on Race, Power and Political Economy at The New School. He continues to inspire through his groundbreaking work in economic justice and equity. But for me, his most enduring legacy will always be the lessons he imparted to me during those formative years. He was the first person to share with me what a liberal arts education was and prompted me to consider the importance of having Black culture on my chosen college campus.

From him introducing me to schools like the University of Pennsylvania, Oberlin (his alma mater), and Wesleyan, I was very intentional about researching selective schools in the northeast with high populations of Black students. I was drawn to Wesleyan not just for its academic rigor and intellectual vibrancy but also for its profound commitment to diversity—especially in its support and affirmation of Black and Latino students. As someone who had often been one of the few Black students in predominantly white educational spaces, I longed to find a community of peers who understood that experience, who had navigated similar challenges, and who were equally eager to leverage their college experience as a springboard to professional opportunities. While I did not love every aspect of my college experience, Darrick Hamilton and Wesleyan University will be included in my eulogy.

Brennan

My personal essay was also about an influential person in my life. I wrote about my older brother, Daron, who was only a year ahead of me in school. We shared a friend group and were in many ways "as thick as thieves," working the same summer job, participating in the same sports, and listening to the same music.

Daron is a typical first child, in many ways exceptional at everything he does and always the responsible one. I was a bit more of a loose cannon and sometimes lacked both motivation and direction academically. While I was a dedicated athlete, my commitment paled in comparison with my older brother's. But I also had areas where I shined in ways that he didn't.

Instead of focusing on our specific accomplishments, my essay was about relationships and my reflections on my place in the world and identity. Growing up in a rural setting where we were not surrounded by peers made family ties even stronger, and I elaborated on why this was meaningful. Though my topic was an influential person in my life, the writing was less about my brother and more about who I wanted to be as an individual, family member, and citizen.

CHAPTER 5

Approaches to Writing—to Prompt or Not to Prompt

At the end of the day, essays are simply a way for colleges to get to know you beyond what may already be evident in other parts of your application. The Common App's seven different essay choices were designed to "prompt" you to see the wide variety of topics you might write about. One of them is even a prompt of your own choosing! Use them to think about what's important to you and what you think colleges should know about you. And remember, there are no right or wrong prompts, and there are no right or wrong answers to them. Your story—whatever it might be—is important.

—Jenny Rickard, President and CEO, Common App

At the start of this book, we admitted that though we are both college counselors and have worked with thousands of students, we do not agree on everything. Our differences come from our different personal and professional experiences and reflect the various writing styles and strategies needed for effective and compelling storytelling. One area where our perspectives split is over the use of essay prompts—whether students should start from the prompts for the personal statement in the Common Application or chart their own path. As you, the applicant, embark on the admission process, we hope this point-counterpoint discussion will help you discover the right method for you based on your writing style and the story you wish to tell.

The Case *Against* Prompts: Brennan's Approach

Let me start with a caveat: some colleges require students to answer specific questions directly, and straying from them can have a negative impact. The University of California's Personal Insight Questions are a prime example, where students must choose from given prompts and answer them succinctly. In such a case, you must follow the directions to the letter. After all, these prompts are designed to elicit desired insights about you that the institutions value.

My advice diverges sharply, however, when it comes to the Common Application personal statement. If you haven't read these essay prompts yet—don't. That's right; ignore them for now. Upon reading the prompts, some students become overwhelmed and boxed in by the language used. Words like *obstacle* or *accomplishment* can cause undue stress as students scramble to find life events that fit these categories, even if those events don't genuinely resonate with them.

I worked with a student once—let's call her Sarah—who was bright, creative, and had a compelling story to tell. But the moment she read the prompt about writing an essay on "overcoming an obstacle," she became fixated on identifying a singular moment of struggle. Weeks passed as she fruitlessly combed through her life for an event that matched the scale she believed the prompt demanded. Her creativity was paralyzed by the constraint she had imposed on herself, all because of a single word in a prompt.

In my experience, students are much more successful when they begin by thinking about their story first. Ask yourself: *What do I want the admission committee to know about me? What is missing from my application that I would like to highlight?* Begin with the story, not the prompt. After you've written a draft, read the prompts and see if your essay naturally aligns with one of them. If not, there's always the last prompt: "topic of your choice." You are not playing a mind game won by guessing which prompt admission officers want you to pick—they truly don't care which one you choose, as long as you tell a meaningful and authentic story. Focus on being yourself.

The Case *For* Prompts: Shereem's Approach

The Common Application prompts are more than just a formality—they are carefully crafted tools designed to help you tap into meaningful stories. Students sitting down without direction often struggle to connect their thoughts into a cohesive narrative. Many end up with an essay that feels disjointed, lacking focus and emotional depth. By selecting a prompt early on, you can give yourself a framework that keeps you anchored, preventing the aimless wandering that leads to frustration.

Writing to a prompt doesn't stifle creativity—it enhances it. With a straightforward question in front of you, you're responding to a challenge. You're no longer faced with the daunting task of simply "writing about yourself"; instead, you're engaging in a structured dialogue with the admission committee. For students who often feel paralyzed by the fear of "not knowing what to write," the prompt becomes a guiding light. It narrows the focus, making the process more manageable and productive.

Moreover, when students choose a prompt and brainstorm within its boundaries, they dive deeper into their reflections. Instead of scattering their thoughts, they zero in on a few essential experiences, exploring them with intentionality and depth. The result is often a more coherent and compelling essay that resonates with the reader.

Brainstorming

If you are looking for perfection in your college essay, search no further. It doesn't exist. In his book *Outliers*, Malcolm Gladwell proposed the "ten-thousand-hour rule," the amount of practice time it takes to master a skill. While you have likely written many essays by your senior year of high school, you are probably a "few" hours short of that threshold. Nonetheless, you can still write a compelling essay, and the more practice the better.

Instead of trying to sit down and write your essay in one shot, spend some time just writing. Make a practice of it. Perhaps you choose to write for 5, 10, or 15 minutes every morning when you wake up or before you go to bed at night. Write about anything that interests or occurs to you. Write to different prompts or react to moments in your life. Challenge some friends to do the same, and take turns coming up with topics/prompts. Just write often.

As writers who journal regularly and always stress the importance of sharing thoughts, ideas, and perspectives, we expect students to have streams of consciousness as they begin to brainstorm for college essay writing. Having a stream of consciousness, in our opinion, means that we allow our brain to go in many different directions and slowly shape those thoughts into what will be a powerful essay.

That's why we are big believers in voice-typing because students can simply talk into their phone or computer and watch the words appear on the screen. These streams of consciousness allow students to get ideas out of their heads, and then they can pick and choose which ones they think they will be most proud of and will support their application. It lets students capture raw, unfiltered thoughts without overthinking, making their essays more authentic and relatable. It also preserves their unique voice, helping them stand out in a sea of similar essays. This technique frees up creativity, breaks writer's block, and leads to unexpected insights by allowing ideas to flow naturally. Writing without structure at first encourages deeper exploration and diverse perspectives, often revealing connections students might have overlooked.

Keeping a record of spontaneous thoughts creates a pool of ideas to pull from when shaping the final essay, ensuring no great detail is lost. It also helps with reflection—students gain a better understanding of their own experiences, leading to more introspective and meaningful writing. This process not only makes the actual writing easier by serving as a rough draft, but it also simplifies revision, making it easier to refine themes and structure. Plus, jotting down thoughts as they come prevents brilliant ideas from slipping away and even helps students process emotions by adding emotional depth that makes essays more impactful.

At its core, this method isn't just about writing—it's about thinking, feeling, and storytelling in the most natural way possible. When students embrace it, they create essays that are more compelling, personal, and memorable to admission officers.

Once you have put in the practice, you are ready for the real thing. Look back over your writing. Are there any vignettes or parts of them that stand out or especially resonate with you? Highlight a sentence or two that you like and try writing a new essay that starts with it.

Once you have gotten down a solid draft of your essay, cut and paste the first and last paragraphs into another document. If you read only those two paragraphs, would you want to read the rest of the essay? Some reviewers will do this to save time when reading applications. Those paragraphs need to grab the reader and make them eager for more. Then, ask yourself what aspects of the paragraphs in between are critical to the message you are hoping to convey. Sometimes applicants unnecessarily repeat themselves in the body of the essay or include filler that is not relevant to the point they are trying to make.

We have worked with too many applicants who get stuck on wanting to write about a specific topic or who have a draft of an essay they badly want to work well, but it just doesn't. Do not be afraid to abandon an ineffective essay and begin anew. Don't spin your wheels.

The Role of Vulnerability in Writing

One of the most effective ways to connect with your reader is through showing vulnerability. Many students believe that their college essays need to showcase only their successes and strengths, but the truth is that admission officers appreciate essays that reveal growth through challenges, mistakes, or moments of doubt.

Vulnerability doesn't mean oversharing or writing about deeply personal traumas you're uncomfortable discussing. Instead, it's about being honest with yourself and your reader. Acknowledging where you've struggled or where you've had to rethink your approach to life can be incredibly powerful as long as it's done thoughtfully and with a clear sense of purpose. Essays demonstrating emotional maturity and introspection often stand out because they feel real and relatable.

The Role of Humor and Personality

Letting your personality shine is another way to stand out in your college essay. While your essay should maintain a level of seriousness, especially when discussing personal growth or important challenges, don't be afraid to weave in humor or lightheartedness if it feels authentic to who you are. If you are not naturally funny, don't try to be. Forced humor or creativity usually doesn't land well.

Final Thoughts on Choosing Your Approach

Let's face it: the college essay is an exercise in self-presentation, and it's tempting to think that abstraction or complexity will make your essay stand out. But we have seen repeatedly that simple, direct responses to prompts often yield the most profound results. Using a prompt isn't about limiting your voice—it's about **guiding it to a place of clarity** where it can be heard clearly by the admission committee.

Whether you respond to a prompt from the start or develop your story before finding a prompt, the most important thing to remember is that your essay should feel like *you*. Admission officers are looking for a window into who you are, how you think, and what you care about. There is no single "right" way to approach the college essay; give yourself the time and space to reflect on your experiences, brainstorm freely, and experiment with different ideas. And above all, trust that your story—told in your voice—is worth sharing. By crafting an essay that speaks to your unique strengths and experiences, you'll be one step closer to finding a college that will allow you to continue growing into the person you're meant to be.

To Parents

You are providing support and encouragement for your child's writing without overshadowing their authentic voice. The most effective college essays come from the student's own reflections and writing. Encourage your child to start brainstorming early, giving them ample time to explore different ideas. You can help by asking thought-provoking questions about their experiences, values, and goals, but resist the urge to dictate the essay's content or style. Your child may need reassurance that their stories are worth telling. Colleges are looking for the student's genuine voice, not a polished adult perspective. Your most valuable contribution will be to create a supportive environment for your child to engage in this vital self-reflection. At best you are a sounding board.

The personal statement is more than just a writing assignment; it's a window into your child's soul, journey, and dreams. Encourage them to reflect on moments that have truly mattered in their lives. For example, we know of one parent shared how their son, who initially struggled with public speaking, found his voice through debate club. This experience became a powerful essay about growth and self-confidence. Guide your child to think beyond grades and extracurriculars, focusing instead on personal anecdotes that reveal their character, values, and passions. Be patient, listen as they explore their ideas, and remind them that vulnerability is a strength.

Let us offer you an example: Superdad David was eager to help his son Adam with his college essay. A successful professional writer, David was tempted to heavily edit Adam's work or rewrite portions to make it "better." However, he recalled advice from a college admission officer and decided to step back. Instead of dictating the essay's direction, David asked Adam thoughtful questions about his experiences and listened attentively. Through these conversations, Adam remembered his transformative experience tutoring younger students in math, a subject he once struggled with himself. This realization led to an essay that authentically portrayed Adam's growth, empathy, and dedication. By resisting the urge to overly influence the essay, David allowed Adam's genuine voice to shine through, resulting in a more impactful and personal statement.

This example illustrates how authentic reflection can lead to powerful essays for students and how supportive but restrained guidance from parents can facilitate this process.

Offer Help with Brainstorming

Here are three way parents can help their student brainstorm ideas for their application essays.

Jogging memory. Sit down with your child and reminisce about various milestones and memorable moments in their life. Often parents remember key events and experiences that their child might have overlooked or forgotten.

Providing perspective. Parents have the advantage of having witnessed their child's growth and development from its start. Share insights on how certain experiences have shaped their character. For instance, if your child faced and overcame a significant challenge, discuss how this experience has influenced their resilience and problem-solving skills.

Identifying strengths and qualities. Sometimes, teenagers struggle to recognize their own strengths. As a parent, you can help identify and articulate these qualities. Whether it's their empathy, determination, creativity, or leadership, your perspective can help highlight these traits through specific anecdotes.

Choose Your Own Adventure

Every writer approaches storytelling differently, and finding the right way to tell your own story is one of the most important parts of writing a successful college essay. Whether you start by tackling essay prompts head-on, brainstorming with family and friends, or carving out your own path entirely, what matters most is that you take ownership of your process. Your essay is your narrative, and you should feel empowered to shape it in a way that feels authentic to you.

That said, writing isn't a straight road—it's more like an unfolding journey where you get to decide the direction. If one approach isn't working, don't hesitate to change course. Maybe you begin with a structured outline but find that freewriting sparks more meaningful ideas. Or perhaps a casual conversation with a friend brings out a personal insight you hadn't considered before. The key is to remain open and flexible, allowing your process to evolve as your ideas take shape.

The best essays often emerge from a willingness to explore different paths before settling on the right one. Just like in a "Choose Your Own Adventure" story (ever heard of those?), where each decision you make—how you brainstorm, what details you include, the tone you take—shapes the final outcome. Some paths may lead to dead ends, but even those missteps can be valuable, revealing what does and doesn't resonate with you as a writer. By experimenting with different approaches, you might uncover a perspective or experience that truly sets your essay apart.

At the same time, don't be afraid to lean on those who know you well. Feedback from teachers, mentors, family, or friends can help you see your story from a fresh angle and refine your message. Writing is rarely a solo endeavor—while your voice should remain at the center, trusted readers can help you sharpen and clarify your ideas.

Ultimately, crafting an essay isn't just about checking a box for college applications; it's about discovering how to tell your own story in the most compelling and truthful way. The more you embrace the adventure of writing—remaining open to new ideas, shifting your approach when needed, and trusting in the process—the more authentic and powerful your final essay will be.

Every writer has their own approach to storytelling. Whether you choose to start with essay prompts, engage family and friends in brainstorming, or chart your own course, it is important for you, the applicant, to own your decision. Don't be afraid to shift your approach if it is not working and to lean on those around you who know you well. Writing is a process, and one that requires openness and flexibility.

CHAPTER 6

No Bad Topics, Just Bad Essays

Who you are, WHY you are, and WHO you want to become are just as important as what you've accomplished. Tell us about yourself.

—Olufemi Ogundele, Associate Vice Chancellor and Dean of Enrollment, University of California, Berkeley

---

Politics, religion, "sex, drugs, and rock & roll." What are the topics that should be avoided in writing a college essay? You will hear a range of opinions on this issue, and we are here to tell you that it is less about *what* you write and more about *how* you write it. We have read essays on every topic imaginable. From the mundane, like an essay on broccoli, to the complex, like the influence of spacecraft aerodynamics on an applicant's academic trajectory.

Honestly, admission officers are less focused on what the topic is and more on what they learn about you. Rarely is the topic notable unless it is written about poorly. We hope to prevent you from doing that. With all of that said, you will hear of topics that are seen as taboo or cliché. It is good to be aware of these, but don't get hung up on this. Instead, focus on how you tell your unique story in a way only you can. For instance, rather than writing about generic experiences like scoring the winning goal in a soccer match or volunteering at a local shelter, delve into the specifics that made those moments significant for you. Reflect on your internal growth, the lessons you learned, and how these experiences shaped your perspective. This depth of insight will reveal the real you, far beyond the surface-level achievements.

Clichés often stem from well-intentioned but overused narratives. For example, many students write about the importance of teamwork through sports or the rewards of community service, which are undeniably valuable experiences. However, these themes become cliché when they lack personal depth and specificity. To avoid falling into this trap, ask yourself: *What makes my experience different from everyone else's?* Perhaps you could focus on an incident during a game where your leadership skills were tested in an unexpected way or on an unforeseen relationship you built with someone while volunteering that influenced your worldview. By highlighting these personal anecdotes, you transform a common theme into a compelling and distinctive story.

Another way to sidestep clichés is to infuse your essay with your voice and perspective. Think about the quirks and characteristics that define you. Are there particular hobbies or interests that set you apart? Maybe your passion for solving complex puzzles has taught you perseverance and patience, or your love for baking has become a metaphor for your approach to problem-solving and creativity. Use these unique elements of your personality to frame your narrative. When you stay true to who you are and express your genuine passions and reflections, you not only avoid clichés but also create a memorable essay that rings with authenticity and originality.

Let's consider some examples of common essay themes and how the same topic can either yield an eye-rolling essay or an impactful one.

The Service Essay

Volunteering one's time in service to others is admirable and signals important character traits that can stand out in admission. "Performing" service to boost one's odds of admission is another matter, however, and is often transparent to admission readers. Students do not need to travel to far-away locales in order to demonstrate their commitment to community and serving others. Look around you; there are likely many needs in your immediate surroundings.

Every year admission offices are flooded with essays about a volunteer experience that applicants had. Unfortunately, many of these essays miss the mark. They often read like a travelogue or appear Pollyannaish, even voyeuristic. A writer might talk about their excursion into a remote village or explain how "just seeing the smiles on their faces" was reward enough. They reek of privilege and can be patronizing in unintended ways. Applicants err in focusing more on the individuals they are serving or the circumstances they find themselves in—"I had never before seen such poverty and despair"—than on reflecting on who they are.

If you are going to write about an experience you have had volunteering, help the reader understand the why behind it and what it says about you, what you value, and how you think about the world around you. There are ways to write about service that don't sound self-righteous or self-congratulatory. How do you know yourself better as a result of the experience, and has it impacted how you view your future studies or interactions?

The Sports Essay

A season-ending injury, a missed goal, or a championship upset—these are frequent themes when students write about the role of athletics in their life. It is almost comical how many of this type of essay admission officers read in any given year. Does that mean you shouldn't write about sports? Not necessarily, but again it's how you write about it that matters.

For many students, a sport represents a significant commitment of time and energy. Before you choose to write about it in your college essay, ask yourself if you are missing an opportunity to talk about another aspect of your life or experience that might not be as apparent in your application. If you are a competitive athlete, it will likely show through in other parts of your application. If you do decide that you are compelled to focus on this aspect of your life, ask yourself what a reader might not know about you on the surface. The danger is that the essay will become more about the athletic pursuit, goal, or injury and less about the kind of person you are. Before that buzzer sounds, make sure you have not run out the clock on what can be shared about your unique perspective or approach.

The Grandparent Essay

The death of a relative, the influence of a grandparent, or caring for an elderly family member can all be meaningful experiences. The most frequent mistake in this type of essay is that the reader emerges having learned more about the grandparent than about the applicant.

This type of essay can work, like when Brennan's son wrote about his relationship with his grandfather in what turned out to be a powerful college essay (described in chapter 3). The key was that after briefly introducing the grandfather, the writer spent the bulk of the essay reflecting on how their relationship made him realize who he was as a young man and how he showed up in the world. He talked about a legacy of storytelling in the family and how that impacted the life he wants to lead.

If you are going to write about a family member or anyone who is not you, make sure you are clear about why you are doing so and make it a mini-autobiography of you, not a mini-biography of them.

The Political Essay

If you choose to write about participating in a political campaign or reflect on your outlook toward a local, national, or international issue, be careful. You might be advised not to write about political topics, but if you are passionate about a political subject, go for it. If it says something about who you are and what you value, you don't need to avoid it.

At the same time, remember that colleges are looking for good community members who will contribute to campus life and welcome diverse perspectives. If you write a political essay that is perceived to be judgmental or close-minded about a social issue, it could rub the reader the wrong way and have unintended consequences.

As you consider an issue that could be politically charged, think less about defending your stance in the essay and more about what this perspective says about you as an individual, learner, and citizen. Check yourself for self-righteousness, and make sure you are not using the essay as a soapbox.

The Religion Essay

You might want to write about the role of spirituality in your life or perhaps about a religiously founded stance on abortion or another sensitive issue. Again, like essays on politics, be careful about not offending a reader who might have a different worldview.

How has religion shaped you or informed your approach to life and relationships? What might a reader not know about faith in your life that would make your application incomplete if they don't understand it? We have read extremely thoughtful reflections on religion and how individuals have internalized or acted on teachings of scripture. On the contrary, we've also read essays that verge on being judgmental. If you choose to write about religion, make sure you are sharing about you and not just scripture.

The Adversity or Trauma Essay

Some students have faced more hardships in their young life than others. If you are one of these applicants, that doesn't mean you should feel obligated to address it in your essay. Likewise, if you have not faced significant adversity, you shouldn't feel compelled to amplify or hype small setbacks you have experienced. Here are common examples of this essay type that can verge on cliché:

- **The immigrant's struggle:** a generalized story about the hardships of immigration without specific, personal details.
- **The disability overcome:** framing a disability solely as an obstacle to overcome rather than a part of one's identity.
- **The childhood adversity surmounted:** a generalized tale of triumphing over a difficult childhood without specific insights.

Of course, if these experiences are an important part of the story you need to tell, then write about them. A general explanation of the circumstances, however, will not be impactful without context for how it has shaped you or contributed to you better understanding yourself and your place in the world.

Remember, the common types of essay topics described above are not inherently bad, but they are written about so frequently by applicants that it's challenging to present them in a fresh, original way. If you choose to write about one of these topics, focus on individualizing details and unique insights to make your essay stand out.

To Parents

"But this is who my kid is! She doesn't have anything else to write about? How can she avoid these if she identifies with one of these?!"

We understand the above concern. This is, verbatim, an email from a mom. It's a common situation that many parents and students face. Here is a response to that mom:

Hi mom of wonderful daughter,

I totally get it—if this experience is who she is, then of course it makes sense that she wants to write about it! The goal isn't to avoid these topics altogether but to make sure her essay feels personal, fresh, and reflective of her rather than just another version of a story admission officers have read a hundred times.

If this experience has truly shaped her, then she should absolutely write about it. The key is making sure she's not just telling the broad, expected version of the story. Instead of focusing on the adversity itself, she can dig deeper into the how—how it shaped her perspective, how it influenced the way she sees herself or others, how it pushed her to grow in ways she might not have expected. The best essays aren't about what happened but about why it mattered and what it changed.

Encourage her to think about the smaller, more personal moments within the bigger story. What's a specific detail or realization she had that might surprise the reader? What's something about her experience that only she could write? If she's writing about immigration, for example, maybe it's not about the challenges of moving to a new country but about a single memory, like the first time she felt at home, or a tiny, unexpected cultural difference that shaped her identity. If it's about overcoming adversity, maybe the real story is in the unexpected part of the journey—the thing she learned about herself that she never would have seen coming.

At the end of the day, it's not about avoiding these topics; it's about making sure they feel real, specific, and deeply personal to her. If she does that, then it won't feel cliché. It'll feel like her story, and that's exactly what colleges want to read.

It's not always about having a completely unique experience but about bringing a unique perspective to that experience. Encourage your daughter to trust her voice and her insights. With careful reflection and honest writing, she can make even a common topic distinctly her own.

This response made all the difference for the mom. She stopped reading all the "best college essays" books and refocused her attention on helping her daughter to examine her life and how it was different from those of her peers.

The daughter recalled a time over a holiday break when she and her mom had stayed up until three in the morning doing a deep dive on Ancestry.com and finding out things about their family they never knew. They were in awe of their family's history and the triumphs and challenges their ancestors had faced. The resulting essay was not about their ancestors but about the time spent together. A middle-aged mom and her teen daughter laughing and learning together while drinking ginger tea and making non-roasted smores in December. Has anyone else ever done that with their child?

Being 1 of 1

Imagine standing in a snow-covered field, each flake falling around you unique in its design. Just like those snowflakes, you are entirely one of a kind. No two snowflakes are alike, and similarly, there is no one else in the world who has the same blend of experiences, talents, dreams, and perspectives as you do. Embracing this idea of being "1 of 1" means recognizing and celebrating your individuality. You are a limited edition, a masterpiece in your own right, and this realization is both empowering and crucial as you navigate the important stages of your life, including the college admission process.

When you start to see yourself as a unique individual, you begin to appreciate the distinctive qualities that make you special. Think about it: your sense of humor, your hobbies, your approach to solving problems, and your journey through life are entirely your own. Maybe you have a passion for painting that allows you to see the world in vibrant colors, or perhaps you have a knack for coding that turns complex problems into elegant solutions. These are not just minor aspects of who you are but rather the core components that define you. Just as no two snowflakes have the same intricate pattern, your traits and experiences form a pattern that is yours alone.

As we discussed in chapter 2, authenticity is key in college applications; admission officers can tell when a student is genuine versus when they are trying to fit a mold. By embracing your unique identity and sharing it honestly, you not only avoid clichés but also create a compelling narrative that resonates with authenticity.

"The piercing flashes of red and blue through the dark night sky as she was led away are etched into my memory."

Prison is probably not the first topic you would expect to read about in a college essay, but I (Brennan) worked with a student whose mother was incarcerated, and she wrote a compelling essay that at once provided important context and was extremely heartwarming, allowing the reader to learn about the young woman and what made her special.

The sections of a college application don't provide a ready space for such information. It doesn't obviously go in the activities section (Family responsibilities: Visiting Mom in jail) or in the personal data section (Mom's employer: State penitentiary), but her mother's incarceration was part of this applicant's lived experience. One might think that writing about a parent being locked up would be something to avoid. The reality is that this essay was not about prison or why the mother was there but was instead about the importance of relationships and perspective in this applicant's eyes.

Spend less time consumed by a search for a "winning" topic. Understand that trying to find a topic never before written about in a college essay is a fool's errand. Most admission officers have read so many applications over their career that you would be hard-pressed to come up with an essay topic they have never encountered before. The key lies not in finding an original topic but in finding your original take on a topic. Focus on the guidance in the chapters to come and on writing well.

CHAPTER 7

Finding Feedback

Stress test your writing for authenticity (which is much more important than grammar, spelling, or writing technique). Read your essay to yourself, out loud and in front of a mirror and ask, "Does this sound like me? Does this build on the rest of my story found in the application?" Or better yet, ask a parent or teacher to read it and ask them the same questions. For the ultimate stress test, ask a friend to read it with these questions in mind—your peers are often the harshest critics!

—Jay Jacobs, Vice Provost for Enrollment Management, University of Vermont

---

Even the best writers have editors. As we have written this book, we have benefited from the ability to coauthor and solicit feedback from each other. Students, we urge you NOT to go at this alone. We have recommended getting feedback in other chapters and have suggested turning to school counselors, other college admission professionals, and even AI (more on this in chapter 12). For your best work to shine, you must know how others are or could be interpreting it. Is all feedback valuable? Not necessarily, but please be open to it while being firm about maintaining your voice.

Proofreading is a necessity. We cannot tell you how many essays we have read where students have accidentally used the wrong word or form of the word and, unfortunately, changed the intent of a thought, sentence, or paragraph. Proofreading can be led by a virtual grammar assistant, an English teacher, a parent, a friend, or a counselor.

When you ask for feedback, consider two points. Our shared mentor, Susan Tree, likes to emphasize the first: "A lack of planning on your part doesn't constitute an emergency on mine." Give your supporters plenty of time to offer feedback. We are talking days or weeks, not minutes or hours! If you wait until the night before the application deadline, it is on you. The other point is to not "shop" your essay around. Not everyone has experience reading college essays, and, often, too many people offering feedback just muddies the waters while diluting your voice. A saying comes to mind: "Too many cooks in the kitchen spoils the broth."

Check Yourself

Before you begin soliciting input from others, stop and check in with yourself.

- How are you feeling about your writing?
- Are you excited about the topic you chose?
- Are you trusting your instincts?
- When you read your essay out loud, does it bring you joy or angst?

If it is the latter, then perhaps you need to go back to the drawing board. If you're not proud of your writing, then getting insight from others is a waste of time.

Read It Out Loud

It may feel awkward at first, and maybe somewhat obvious, but one of the best ways to determine whether your voice is coming through in your writing is to actually use your voice. Once you have a solid draft, read it out loud. Sometimes, when we read a piece we have written, we add in words or punctuation that isn't on the screen/paper but is in our heads. When we put voice to it, everything is exposed. Go the extra step, record yourself reading it, and play it back to see what is missing, overdone, or awkwardly expressed.

Stranger Test

It is important to have someone who knows you read your writing because they might be aware of things you left out or parts that don't sound like you. It can be equally as useful to have a complete stranger give you feedback because your ultimate audience (the admission reader) will likewise have no background knowledge of you. Ask your parents to share your essay with a friend or colleague who has never met you, with instructions to read the piece and then summarize what they learned about you in two to three sentences. Also have them give three adjectives that they think capture who you are after having read your statement. Did your intended message come across in their summary? Do the adjectives they identified line up with what you are trying to show about yourself? Try this with a few different strangers to see if there is agreement across their reactions.

Drop Everything

Imagine that you and 20 classmates turned in college essays to your English teacher without putting your name on them, and the teacher dropped them all on the floor. If your teacher or a classmate picked yours up and read it, would they know it was you? If not, it is too generic. Could anyone else have written your essay? If so, you are missing an opportunity. Go ahead: try it with your class!

Keep It Positive

Give your essay to someone and instruct them to give you only positive feedback after reading it. Even if they have constructive criticism, ask them to save that for a later time and focus on what resonates or stands out as compelling in the writing. Doing this lets you focus on what works and how your writing connects with the reader. You can tell by the amount of positive feedback you receive whether or not it is a compelling piece.

Sentence Success

Pick out your favorite three to five sentences in your essay before passing it to another. Ask your reader to do the same. Do you agree on which sentences are your favorites? Discuss your picks with your reader and ask them why they chose the sentences they did. Consider taking one or two of the sentences chosen and starting a new essay with them if you find yourself dissatisfied with the essay you shared.

More or Less

Try to adhere to the "smart brevity" concept when writing your college essay. Journalists use this style of writing to cut to the heart of an issue. What is essential in your writing? The idea is that, often, less is more when trying to communicate a point. This is especially true when an admission reader has limited time and might be skimming your essay. Ask your feedback partner to identify what parts of the essay are crucial to the message you're trying to send. Ask them also to underline any parts of the essay that seem extraneous to your thesis or to the story you're telling. Try removing those parts from the essay and see how it reads as a result.

You Do You

We have suggested a number of strategies for soliciting feedback on your writing. We are not suggesting that you try all of these approaches, because too much input can be more confusing than correcting. Consider what has worked for you in your academic work.

- Is it easier for you to incorporate feedback from your peers or from an adult in your life?
- Are you often defensive about your own work?

Figure these things out before you start asking for help, as any assistance you get will only be as good as you are willing to hear.

Let's face it—no one likes being told their work isn't perfect, especially when that work involves pouring your heart out on paper for something as nerve-wracking as a college essay. You've spent hours, maybe even days, crafting what you believe is a compelling narrative, only to have someone else pick it apart. Ouch. But here's the thing: getting suggestions for revision is both a necessary evil and, believe it or not, one of the best gifts you can receive during the college admission process.

Imagine this: You've just finished the first draft of your essay, and you're feeling pretty good. You've hit all the points you wanted to cover, your story is there, and maybe you've even thrown in a clever metaphor or two. But something doesn't feel quite right. It's like when you're baking a cake and everything seems perfect, but it doesn't rise as expected. That's where feedback comes in—it's the secret ingredient that can take your essay from decent to delicious.

Feedback: The Secret Sauce Your Essay Needs

Consider the case of Emma. She was a student who came to me (Shereem) with an essay, which she was sure was a home run. She'd written about her passion for environmental science, detailing her volunteering hours. It was heartfelt and full of action—but it was missing something. Initially, the essay was a lot of *what* and *how* without enough *why*. She was so focused on showing what she did that she forgot to explain why environmental science mattered to her personally.

When I pointed this out, Emma was initially resistant; she felt like she'd done everything right. But after some reflection (and maybe a little grumbling), she realized that the essay needed more depth. She added a story about how a childhood trip to the Grand Canyon sparked her love for the environment. Suddenly, the essay had context; it had a soul. The feedback hadn't changed the story—it had sharpened it, making it more focused, personal, and compelling.

And here's the thing about feedback. Embracing criticism is part of the writing process and is one of the best ways to grow as a writer and thinker. It's like going to the gym: you won't get stronger if you never try a weight heavier than the one with which you started. You need to push yourself and challenge your limits, and sometimes, that means facing the discomfort of criticism.

When you get feedback, especially from someone who knows what they're talking about—whether that's a teacher, a school counselor, or an experienced college admission advisor—you can see your work from a different perspective. These people aren't trying to tear you down but are helping you build something better. They're offering you the benefit of their experience, knowledge, and understanding of what makes an essay stand out.

And let's not forget, these folks have seen a lot of essays. They know what works and doesn't, what resonates with admission officers and what falls flat. They can spot clichés from a mile away and know whether a story sounds authentic or forced. Their aim is not to rewrite your essay for you; they want to help you see what you might have missed, push you to dig a little deeper, and guide you in making your essay the best it can be.

Use our S.U.C.C.E.S.S. checklist when reviewing your essay

S - Storytelling
Ensure your essay tells a compelling and personal story. Share a unique experience or perspective that showcases your individuality.

U - Uniqueness
Highlight what makes you different and one-of-a-kind. Discuss your cultural background, lived experiences, and individual strengths.

C - Clarity
Write clearly and concisely. Make sure your essay is well organized and easy to follow.

C - Connection
Connect your experiences and insights to your future goals and aspirations. Explain how your past has prepared you for college and beyond.

E - Emotions
Share your feelings and reflections to evoke emotions in your reader. Be authentic, vulnerable, and honest in your writing.

S - Specificity
Use specific examples and details to illustrate your points. Avoid vague statements and generalizations.

S - Strengths
Highlight your strengths and how they have developed through your experiences. Show how these strengths will contribute to your success in college.

PART III

The Rest of Writing

CHAPTER 8

Supplemental Writing

Essay and short answer responses bring personality and perspective to an application, allowing admissions professionals to get beyond the facts, figures, and statistics to better understand the individual who is applying and what they might bring to a campus community. Such supplemental writing hints at a student's ability to express themselves, but more importantly, offers a window into their way of thinking.

—Eric Maguire, Vice President for Enrollment, Wake Forest University

The additional writing that applicants are asked to submit comes in many forms and can be either required or optional. Even when it is presented as optional, we strongly recommend that students embrace this opportunity to expand on what makes them distinct and why they are qualified for admission.

A supplement is an essay that some colleges ask for in addition to the personal statement. These essays have prompts related to the college's characteristics, programs, priorities, or values. Too often, applicants treat these essays as an afterthought, investing significant time in the personal statement, only to fire off a supplemental essay in the final days or hours before submission. Not a good approach! In this chapter we discuss the common categories of supplemental essays you may encounter and recommendations for how to approach them.

Purposes behind the supplemental writing required by some colleges

Demonstrating interest
Lets applicants show genuine interest in, and knowledge of, the college, indicating why they are a good fit for that specific institution.

Assessing fit
Helps the college evaluate how well an applicant's goals, values, and interests align with its mission, academic programs, and culture.

Highlighting specific attributes
Allows applicants to emphasize aspects of their background, achievements, or aspirations that are particularly relevant or sought after by the college.

Providing additional insight
Offers another opportunity for applicants to showcase their writing skill, creativity, and ability to think critically about important topics or questions.

Differentiating applicants
Helps the college distinguish between similarly qualified applicants by providing more context for an applicant's defining qualities and potential contributions to the campus community.

Why Us Essay

One type of supplemental essay asks applicants to explain the reasons why they are interested in attending the college in question and how they see themselves fitting into, and benefiting from, the college's offerings.

Example: Tufts University

"I am applying to Tufts because . . ."

Considerations

- **Programs and courses:** Mention particular programs, courses, or academic opportunities that align with your interests and career goals.
- **Faculty:** Name professors there whose work you admire and under whom you hope to study.
- **Campus resources:** Highlight specific facilities, research opportunities, study abroad programs, or extracurricular activities that appeal to you.
- **Experiences:** Relate personal experiences or anecdotes that demonstrate your genuine interest in the college.
- **Goals:** Explain how the college's offerings align with your long-term goals and how you envision your future while there.
- **Values and culture:** Discuss how the college's values, culture, or mission resonate with you and how you see yourself fitting into the campus community.
- **Contributions:** Describe how you will contribute to the college, whether through academics, extracurricular activities, community service, or other means.

Although "why us" essays can often be partly recycled for multiple schools, beware of two pitfalls: (1) making the essay too generic and (2) failing to replace school-specific information when reworking your essay.

Intended Major Essay

Another type of supplemental essay asks applicants to explain their chosen field of study, why they are interested in it, and how they have prepared for it.

Example: Carnegie Mellon University

"Most students choose their intended major or area of study based on a passion or inspiration that's developed over time—what passion or inspiration led you to choose this area of study?"

Considerations

- **Insight into academic interests:** Provide the college with an understanding of your academic passions and intellectual curiosity.
- **Demonstrated commitment:** Show your dedication and long-term interest in a particular field, indicating that you are a focused and motivated student.
- **Preparation and readiness:** Highlight your relevant experiences, such as coursework, extracurricular activities, internships, or personal projects, that demonstrate your preparedness for the major.

Context and Community Essay

You might be asked to write about issues like identity, culture, race, politics, or religion. In the wake of the US Supreme Court's decision to strike down race-conscious admission as a "check box" process, the college admission landscape has changed. Yet this ruling does not diminish the importance of your identity, your background, and the unique experiences that have shaped you. Most colleges and universities remain deeply committed to understanding how your personal journey and cultural context have influenced your worldview, your approach to learning, and how you might contribute to the vibrant fabric of their campus community. Essentially, colleges want to gain further insight into your lived experiences and how you feel about, and have been exposed to (or not), difference. How has this impacted you?

Let's be clear: colleges know that this question will make some students uncomfortable. Some people believe that "diversity" does not apply to them. But that's the point. Colleges want students to understand that racial, religious, cultural, and socioeconomic diversity on their campus is real. They need students to understand that classrooms, dorm rooms, dining facilities, and social events will have collections of people who may not look like or think like them, and THAT'S OK! One of the huge drawbacks of the Supreme Court's decision to eliminate race-conscious admission is that college campuses may lose valuable opportunities to bridge cultures. College is a place of learning and exposure, and when colleges ask questions about diversity, they prepare students for their campus mission of access and equality.

Many supplemental essay questions reflect an institution's commitment to diversity by weaving inquiries about race, ethnicity, and identity into broader prompts. These questions may come in various forms, some more direct than others, but they all share a common goal: to understand the factors that have shaped who you are and how you perceive the world around you from a racial or cultural standpoint. For instance, you might be asked to describe the community in which you were raised, discuss how your background has influenced your perspective on diversity and inclusion, or respond to a quotation or contemporary issue.

Example: University of Virginia

"What about your individual background, perspective, or experience will serve as a source of strength for you or those around you at UVA? Feel free to write about any past experience or part of your background that has shaped your perspective and will be a source of strength, including but not limited to those related to your community, upbringing, educational environment, race, gender, or other aspects of your background that are important to you. (250 words)"

Considerations

Reflect deeply on your identity and experiences. Begin by taking time to be introspective. Consider the various dimensions of your identity—race, ethnicity, socioeconomic status, religion, gender, sexual orientation, family background, and any other aspects that are meaningful to you. Reflect on how these elements of your identity have shaped your experiences, values, and outlook on life. Think about the specific moments or challenges that have been pivotal in your personal development.

What aspects of your identity do you consider most defining?

How have these aspects influenced your interactions with others or understanding of the world?

Can you identify specific experiences that illustrate your journey of self-discovery or growth from a cultural standpoint?

Examine your community and its influence. Next, consider the community or communities in which you were raised. This could be your neighborhood, school, cultural group, or any other collective that has been significant in your life. Reflect on the values, traditions, challenges, and opportunities within these communities. Think about how they have shaped your identity and how you have engaged with, or been impacted by, the diversity (or lack thereof) within them.

What are the defining characteristics of your community?

How has your community influenced your understanding of diversity, equity, and inclusion?

Have you contributed to or been impacted by any community initiatives, events, or challenges?

Connect your experiences to broader themes. Now, draw connections between your personal experiences and societal issues. Consider how your story fits into broader conversations about politics, race, identity, diversity, and community. This step is about situating your personal narrative within a context of social change, cul-

How does your personal experience reflect broader social or cultural themes?

What have you learned from navigating your identity in diverse (or homogenous) environments?

How might your experiences inform your contributions to a diverse college campus?

tural dialogue, or historical challenges. It's about showing that you are not only aware of these issues but that you've also thought critically about your place within them.

You can thoughtfully and intelligently respond to questions about race, politics, religion, and diversity, offering admission committees a nuanced and compelling portrait of who you are and how you will contribute to their campus community. This approach not only demonstrates your self-awareness and critical thinking but also highlights the depth and richness of your experiences, ensuring that your application stands out in a competitive admission process.

Character and Creativity

Some supplemental essay questions seek to gauge your creative flair and others to probe the fortitude of your character. Colleges want to admit students who will enliven classroom discourse and who will contribute to the welfare of the campus and care about those around them.

Example: University of Pennsylvania

"*Write a short thank-you note to someone you have not yet thanked and would like to acknowledge.* (We encourage you to share this note with that person, if possible, and reflect on the experience!)"

Institutional Mission and Priorities in Supplemental Essays

When colleges craft supplemental essay prompts, they often align them with their **institutional mission**, **values**, and **priorities**.

What This Means

This means that certain essay questions are designed to assess how well an applicant's values, goals, and interests match what the college stands for. These essays go beyond academics; they probe into a student's potential contributions to the sort of community the college aspires to be.

Here are some examples of how institutional mission might manifest itself in a supplemental essay prompt.

- **Jesuit universities** (e.g., Georgetown, Boston College, Loyola Marymount) often ask about service, ethics, or social justice, as these align with their commitment to education of the whole person and community engagement.
- **STEM-focused institutions** (e.g., MIT, Caltech, Georgia Tech) may have essays focused on problem-solving, innovation, and collaboration in scientific fields.
- **Liberal arts colleges** (e.g., Amherst, Swarthmore, Bowdoin) might ask about intellectual curiosity, interdisciplinary learning, or the importance of discussion-based learning.
- **Diversity-focused institutions** (e.g., Howard, Oberlin, University of California system schools) often prompt students to reflect on personal identity, cultural background, or experiences that contribute to a diverse community.

Why This Is Important

Demonstrates fit. Colleges want students who will thrive in their environment. By aligning your response with their mission, you demonstrate that you have researched the school thoroughly and understand what it values.

Shows commitment and interest. A well-crafted response to a mission-driven prompt signals genuine enthusiasm for the institution. Schools prefer students who truly *want* to be there—not just those applying because of ranking or prestige.

Helps a college shape its community. Schools are intentional about building a diverse, engaged, and mission-driven student body. A supplemental essay helps admission officers identify students who will contribute meaningfully to campus life and uphold the institution's priorities.

How to Use This to Your Advantage

By crafting a thoughtful response that connects your background and ambition with a school's institutional priorities, you demonstrate not only your suitability for the school but also your potential to contribute to its community. Here are some tips for how to make this connection:

- **Research the school's mission statement, values, and strategic priorities**, often found on its website under "About Us" or "President's Message."
- **Identify current events, programs, initiatives, or aspects of campus life** that align with your experiences and goals.
- **Use specific examples** from your life that show how you embody the school's stated values.

Short Answers

Some colleges ask short, pithy questions that invite students to "think quick" or have a little fun. These questions might seem lighthearted, but they serve an important purpose in the admission process. Let us explain why they're part of the application and how you should approach them.

First, these questions break up the monotony of the application. Admission officers read thousands of applications, and after a while, the essays and résumés can start to blend together. A quirky or fun question offers a refreshing change of pace for both you and the admission committee. It's a moment to show your personality in a way that's less formal and more spontaneous than other parts of the application.

Second, answers to these questions are rarely evaluated in the same way your personal essay or academic achievements are. Admission officers don't use them to measure your intellectual prowess or ability to craft a perfect essay. Instead, they're looking for a glimpse into how you think, what makes you smile, or what sparks your curiosity. It's about giving them brief insight into the real you—the person behind the course grades and test scores.

I (Shereem) remember counseling a student named Rebecca through the short-answer portion of her application. Rebecca was brilliant but also serious and meticulous. When she saw a prompt asking her to "describe yourself as an ice cream flavor," she got stuck. She was so used to writing polished, profound essays that the idea of answering something so seemingly trivial felt almost beneath her. But I reminded her that this was a chance to loosen up and have some fun. After some brainstorming, she chose rocky road and explained that, like the flavor, she was a mix of smooth and tough, with a few surprises thrown in—just like her life journey.

The response was simple, but it was also genuine and memorable. Rebecca wasn't trying to impress anyone with a perfect answer; she was just being herself. That's the point of short-answer questions. They're not about the perfect response but about revealing a side of you that might not come through in the more serious or structured parts of your application.

So, as you tackle these fun, quick questions, let them be a moment to show your wit, your humor, or just a little slice of what makes you, you. Embrace the opportunity to be playful, and don't overthink it. Sometimes, the best answer is the one that comes naturally. Here are some examples:

University of Maryland (650 characters or fewer each)

1. If I could travel anywhere, I would go to . . .
2. The most interesting fact I ever learned from research was . . .
3. In addition to my major, my academic interests include . . .
4. My favorite thing about last Friday was . . .
5. Something you might not know about me is . . .

University of Southern California (100 characters or fewer unless noted differently)

1. Describe yourself in three words (25 characters each)
2. What is your favorite snack?
3. Best movie of all time
4. Dream job
5. If your life had a theme song, what would it be?
6. Dream trip
7. What TV show will you binge watch next?
8. Which well-known person or fictional character would be your ideal roommate?
9. Favorite book
10. If you could teach a class on any topic, what would it be?

Stanford University (1–3: 100-word minimum and a 250-word maximum; 4–6: 50-word limit)

1. The Stanford community is deeply curious and driven to learn in and out of the classroom. Reflect on an idea or experience that makes you genuinely excited about learning.
2. Virtually all of Stanford's undergraduates live on campus. Write a note to your future roommate that reveals something about you or that will help your roommate—and us—get to know you better.
3. Please describe what aspects of your life experiences, interests and character would help you make a distinctive contribution as an undergraduate to Stanford University.

4. What is the most significant challenge that society faces today?
5. How did you spend your last two summers?
6. Briefly elaborate on one of your extracurricular activities, a job you hold, or responsibilities you have for your family.

Lists

Are you ready to have a little fun? Some colleges and universities provide space in their writing section for you to be you in a more creative way. Here is one example:

Wake Forest University

1. List five books you've read that have intrigued you.
2. Give us your Top Ten list. (The choice of theme is yours.) (limit: 100 characters per line)

Wake Forest University is renowned for its distinctive "Top Ten" list, a signature element of its application that prompts students to share a list of their favorite things—whether films, experiences, places, or anything else that resonates personally. This isn't just a playful exercise; it's a deliberate strategy to peel back the layers of the applicant's personality, offering admission officers a snapshot of the individual behind the accolades and achievements.

The "Top Ten" list serves as a refreshing departure from the conventional narrative-driven essays that dominate most college applications. Wake Forest understands that students are multifaceted, with interests and quirks that often don't fit neatly into a traditional essay format. By asking for a list, the school is inviting you to reveal those less obvious, but equally significant, aspects of who you are. It's an invitation to showcase your unique perspective, your passions, and the eclectic mix of things that inspire you or bring you joy.

Approaching Wake Forest's "Top Ten" list or any similar prompt requires a blend of quirkiness, creativity, and strategic thinking. Here's how to navigate it:

Curate with intention. This isn't just a laundry list of your favorite things. Each item should be carefully selected to offer a glimpse into a different facet of your personality. For instance, if you include a favorite book, think about what that choice says about your intellectual curiosity or your values. If you mention a favorite place, consider how it reflects your sense of belonging or your cultural identity.

Be thoughtfully unexpected. Don't shy away from including items that might seem unconventional or unexpected. Admission officers appreciate originality, and your willingness to embrace the idiosyncratic can make your application stand out. If your favorite film is a lesser-known indie flick rather than a blockbuster hit, that choice might spark a reader's curiosity and offer a deeper insight into your taste and character.

Balance lightness with depth. While the prompt encourages a certain level of playfulness, it's essential to strike a balance. Your list can (and should) include items that are lighthearted and fun, but consider peppering in choices that carry more depth or significance. This duality shows that you're someone who can appreciate life's simple pleasures while also engaging with more profound ideas.

Reflect; don't perform. It's tempting to craft a list that you think the admission committee wants to see. Resist this urge. The "Top Ten" list is an opportunity for self-reflection, not a performance. Admission officers are adept at sensing when students are trying too hard to impress, so focus on being honest and true to yourself.

Overall, supplemental writing is required for the benefit of the applicant by allowing additional writing to be evaluated in the admission decision. Yes, schools like to know that applicants are curious and insightful, but writing supplement essays is something students should see as a chance to shine above and beyond the personal essay.

CHAPTER 9

Additional Information Section

In a selective admission process, admission committees are trying to learn more about applicants and the context in which they have achieved. Using the additional information section to share more information about their personal experience, background, opportunities, or challenges helps admission committees make more informed admission decisions.

—Ronné P. Turner, Vice Provost for Admissions and Financial Aid, Washington University in St. Louis

---

To write or not to write, that is the question! As with many other questions in college admission, the answer is "it depends" for the part called "Additional Information" (or the like) in the application. While most parts of the college application require a response, there are a few optional spaces to share one's voice.

Optional is the operative word here, which often leads to uncertainty for students trying to put their best foot forward. The Additional Information space in the writing section of the application provides an opportunity to expand on something you touched on in another part of the form or to introduce new information, involvement, or experiences that are not captured elsewhere in the application. So, should you take the opportunity or not?

There is an old—and not so kind—saying among admission officers from the days of paper applications, when all the materials submitted by and for a student would be compiled in one folder: "The thicker the file, the thicker the student." In other words, the more pages of material needed to make the case for a student's candidacy, the more admission officers would assume the student is making up for some gap or deficiency. So, say what you need to in the application—to make sure the admission office fully understands your context, values, strengths, interests, experiences, and potential—but don't overdo it. Consider the following examples of when to use or not to use the Additional Information section.

Extracurriculars

Omit

- You filled all 10 spaces provided in the activities section but you were not able to add your participation in the ping pong club in ninth grade.
- You ran out of space in the explanation for your volunteer work to mention every organization where you have served.

Include

- You were involved in organizing a student-led conference on collaborative political discourse, but there was not enough space in the drop-down menus to explain the scope and scale of the program and your role in it.
- You completed an Eagle Scout or Gold Award project and the project's impact needs more explanation.

Experiences

Omit

- You have traveled extensively with your family and want to list all the countries.

- Your club soccer team won the state championship three times in a row. (Put this information instead in the description or honors of the extracurricular section.)

Include

- You had the opportunity to be involved in a community program that is distinct to your town and needs more explanation in terms of what it is and your role in it.
- A presidential candidate spoke at your high school, and you were able to serve on the planning committee and introduce the candidate. You could expand on what you learned and why it was important to your future goals.

Interests

Omit

- You skateboard occasionally in your free time. (They don't need to know that unless you helped to build a skate park in your community or took some other initiative.)
- You have achieved the highest level in the video game you play daily. (Congratulations on this accomplishment, but they don't need to know.)

Include

- This is the place to put a hobby or interest that doesn't easily fit into the extracurricular section or needs more explanation. An example might be a passion you have for weaving that includes participation in a weaver's guild in which you are the youngest member by 30 years. You might want to share how this hobby developed and the depth of your involvement.
- You helped found the local Explorers program with your town's fire department. You may want to share what moti-

vated you and a few takeaways about what you learned from helping to start an organization like this.

Explanations

Omit

- You took two Advanced Placement courses in both junior and senior years because your school limits the number of advanced courses in which a student can enroll. (This information on enrollment restrictions will already be explained in the school profile provided by your high school.)
- You are a three-season athlete and, therefore, have not had the opportunity to be involved in other after-school activities. (You don't need to tell them this, as it will be obvious based on your sports commitments listed under activities in the application.)

Include

- If a scheduling conflict in your senior year made it impossible to continue studying a foreign language or to take the highest level of math while also enrolling in the political science course you wanted.
- You lost a close relative during your sophomore year and missed a significant amount of school, resulting in lower grades.

Context

Omit

- You are an only child and, therefore, have been primarily surrounded by adults as you have grown up. (This information will be shared where you are asked on the Common Application whether you have any siblings.)

- You moved to another state in elementary school. (Unless it had a significant impact on your family or current situation, you don't need to share this.)

Include

- If you have had responsibilities at home that prevented you from being as involved as you would have liked in athletics or after-school activities. This could be an excellent space to explain how these responsibilities have impacted you.
- You are the first in your family to apply to college and have sought support. If something about this experience has been meaningful or challenging, this might be the place to explain more about it.

If You Use It

We hope you now have a sense of whether you might take advantage of this optional writing space. The *how* is just as important here. Too often, applicants put immense time and energy into crafting, drafting, and proofing the personal statement and supplemental essays, only to undo any good impression they have made by writing lackluster and error-filled additional information.

Less is often more. You don't want to create more work for the admission officer by writing multiple paragraphs when a few bullet points will do the job. Be concise but complete. Ensure you are not repeating information in the optional part that you have provided elsewhere in the application. Write out what you need to communicate; then have a counselor or other supporter read what you have and reflect on what it adds to your candidacy. If you decide to include it, make sure you proofread it.

Remember: this is an *optional* section; most applicants leave it blank. Use it if it provides important context, but don't feel compelled to.

CHAPTER 10

Other Writing in an Application

Talking about your activities within the application is an opportunity to give colleges a deeper understanding of what you value and where you find delight. There's a lot to glean from how you choose to spend your time. It's a chance for us to get a glimpse of what brings you joy; what challenges and excites you. So don't just tell us what you've done. Tell us why you've done it. This can provide great insight into how you might engage and contribute when you become part of our community.

—Ingrid W. Hayes, Senior Vice President for Enrollment Management, Spelman College

While the personal statement and supplemental essays may be the primary vehicle through which you show your abilities as a writer, there are other ways that you may have the opportunity—or be required—to express yourself. Remember, everything you enter into your application and the interactions you have with the admission office reflect back on you, so be sure to give the time and energy that these other areas deserve.

Activities Section

The Activities section of your college application is your opportunity to showcase the depth of your involvement beyond the classroom.

It's not just a list of clubs and your positions in them—it's a strategic chance to highlight your passions, your leadership, and the unique contributions you've made to your community. Colleges are looking for more than just academic achievers; they want to admit well-rounded individuals who bring character, diverse experiences, and a strong sense of purpose to campus.

With the Common Application allowing only 100 characters for the name of the organization, 50 characters to explain your position, and 150 characters to describe the activity, every word counts. It might feel like trying to squeeze a novel into a tweet, but this constraint forces you to be clear, concise, and impactful. The key is to think of this section as a set of bullet points on a résumé. You're not just listing what you did; you're emphasizing what you accomplished, how you showed initiative, and why it mattered. Start by identifying your most significant activities—those that reflect your interests and values—as this is meant to be a prioritized list. Follow the directions!

Position/Leadership

If you held a leadership role, use the 50 characters to convey not just the title but also the level of responsibility. For example, instead of just putting "President," you could write "President of the Environmental Club, led a 20-member team." This provides context and highlights your role in a meaningful way. Don't exaggerate your position. Listing your chore of taking out the trash under family responsibilities as "Waste Management Consultant" is going to induce eye-rolling.

Organization Name

Properly identifying the activity gives a first impression, so don't get lazy or overly creative in naming it. Avoid acronyms that the admission office will not recognize, especially if they are specific to your school. While YMCA is generally known because it is a national organization, EVO (your school's **E**nvironmental **V**iability **O**rganization, say) will be meaningless without the full name.

Description

In the 150-character description, focus on impact. Quantify your achievements when possible: Did you organize a fundraising event that raised $5,000? Did you lead a project that increased participation by 30%? Be specific, but also be strategic—choose details that align with the qualities you want to emphasize.

Ultimately, the Activities section is about telling a story of your growth and contributions. When done well, it gives admission officers a glimpse into your world, showing them not just what you've done but who you are. Be authentic, be precise, and remember: this is your chance to make your application come alive.

Change of Schools, Disciplinary Action, and Extraordinary Circumstances

Whether it's changing schools, dealing with health issues, or facing disciplinary action, these interruptions can be challenging. However, they also offer opportunities for growth and self-reflection.

When responding to prompts about these interruptions, it's important to be honest, concise, and focused on how you've grown. Consider how the different emotions and experiences you've encountered have contributed to your personal development and helped you navigate complex changes in life.

Life doesn't always go according to plan. Sometimes, circumstances beyond our control—or even those within it—disrupt the progress of our education.

Reflect on the Circumstances and Impact

Admission officers want to understand the context of your experience, how it affected you, and what you learned from it. This reflection shows maturity and self-awareness.

- **Describe the circumstances:** Clearly explain the situation. Was it a move that disrupted your education, a health challenge, or a disciplinary issue? Be straightforward and factual without dwelling on unnecessary details.
- **Assess the impact:** Reflect on how this event or situation affected your academic journey, your emotions, and your personal development. What were the immediate and long-term effects?

Example: If you had to change schools due to a family move, describe how this affected your social life, academic performance, and emotional well-being.

Explain the Challenges and How You Overcame Them

This is your opportunity to show resilience and growth. Admission officers are looking for evidence that you can adapt, evolve, and come out stronger on the other side.

- **Detail the challenges:** Explain the specific challenges you faced during this time. Were there academic struggles, emotional hardships, or social difficulties?
- **Keep it tight:** Be concise in describing the circumstances. It is easy to digress and include more information than is needed.
- **Show how you overcame them:** Discuss the strategies you used to overcome these challenges. Did you seek help from a counselor, develop new study habits, or find a support system?

Example: If you faced disciplinary action, you could explain how this experience made you reevaluate your choices and what steps you took to improve your behavior, such as participating in counseling or getting involved in positive extracurricular activities.

Highlight Lessons Learned

Admission officers are interested in seeing how you've grown from your experiences. This is where you can demonstrate maturity, responsibility, and a forward-looking attitude.

- **Identify key lessons:** Reflect on what you've learned from the experience. Have you become more resilient, empathetic, or self-aware?
- **Show how you've applied these lessons:** Discuss how these lessons have influenced your behavior, choices, and mindset moving forward. How have you ensured that you won't face similar challenges again?

Example: If you changed schools, you might write about the lessons of adaptability and engaging in new communities. If you faced disciplinary action, you might highlight what you learned about the impact of your behavior on those around you.

Craft a Clear and Honest Narrative

Your response should be direct and sincere. Colleges appreciate honesty, but they also value applicants who can communicate their stories clearly and concisely.

- **Be honest:** Don't try to sugarcoat the situation or make excuses. Acknowledge what happened and take responsibility where appropriate.
- **Be concise:** Stick to the facts and focus on the outcome. There's no need for an overly dramatic retelling—just the truth and its impact on you. This is not a creative writing exercise.
- **Show positivity:** While it's important to acknowledge the difficulties, also highlight the positive outcomes and the ways you've moved forward.

Example: If you were suspended for a lapse in judgment, you could explain what led to that decision, the immediate consequences, and how you've since made changes to your behavior. Emphasize the lesson learned and how it has made you more thoughtful and responsible.

Sample Essay: Change of Schools

Prompt: Explain how changing schools impacted your high school experience, the challenges you faced, and what you learned from the experience.

When I was 14, my family moved from Chicago to a small town in Oregon, uprooting me from the only home I'd ever known. The change felt monumental, and I experienced a whirlwind of emotions—fear, sadness, and confusion—each fighting for dominance as I adjusted to my new reality.

The first few months at my new school were the hardest. I was the new kid in a small, tight-knit community where everyone seemed to have known each other since kindergarten. Socially, I felt like an outsider, and academically, I struggled to catch up to my peers, who had had different curricula. The challenge was overwhelming, and I saw my grades slip for the first time in my life.

Gradually, I learned to face the challenges head-on. I sought help from my teachers, who offered extra support, and I joined the school's debate club, where I found a group of friends who shared my interests. These actions didn't just help me adapt; they taught me resilience, self-advocacy, and the value of stepping out of my comfort zone.

By the end of that year, I had not only caught up academically but also found a place within the school community. The experience taught me that change, while daunting, can lead to growth and new opportunities. Moving forward, I approach challenges with a mindset of adaptability, embracing change and growth.

Communication Outside the Application

Students should seriously consider communicating with colleges of interest apart from the application itself. When done strategically, this can be both effective and impactful. The key, however, is knowing when and how to do it.

Communicating with colleges beyond submitting an application can be beneficial in two ways. First, it shows demonstrated interest. Admission officers want to admit students who are genuinely excited about their school, and thoughtful communication can reflect that enthusiasm. Second, it allows you to personalize your relationship with the college. Instead of being just another name in a stack of applications, you become a real person with known interests, questions, and a proactive approach.

When should you reach out to a college? Here are some opportune moments:

After visiting campus: If you've visited the campus or attended a virtual event, sending a follow-up email thanking the admission representative and mentioning something specific you learned or appreciated can reinforce your interest. When you are on campus, collect the business card or contact information from those individuals you meet and ask who your regional admission officer is, if applicable.

To ask thoughtful questions: If you have specific questions about a program, department, or opportunities at the college that aren't easily answered on the website, reaching out shows that you're doing your homework and are seriously considering how the school aligns with your goals.

To update on new achievements: If something significant happens after you've submitted your application—like winning an award, completing a major project, or taking on a leadership role—sending a brief email to update your admission officer can add enrich your application. You do not need to do this for each new piece of information; we recommend that you wait, when possible, and send one comprehensive update.

When deferred or wait-listed: If you are deferred during early admission or placed on the waiting list, then sending the admission office a well-crafted letter of continued interest can be a crucial way to express your ongoing desire to attend the school and provide any updates since your application.

This kind of communication can be bothersome for the recipient if it's excessive or lacks substance. Admission offices are busy, and sending frequent, unnecessary emails can come off as overbearing. Avoid repeating information that's already in your application or asking generic questions that could be easily answered with a little research of available information.

Communicating with colleges outside of your application can be highly effective when done thoughtfully. It's your chance to make a memorable impression, demonstrate your genuine interest, and build a connection with the admission team. Just remember to be strategic, respectful, and purposeful in your interactions.

CHAPTER 11

Letters of Recommendation

A well-crafted letter of recommendation offers a nuanced view of a student's character and academic potential that might not be fully captured through grades and test scores alone. It helps us see the student in a broader context, adding depth to their application and providing insight into their contributions to their community and potential impact on our campus.

—Mark Butt, Director of Undergraduate Admission, Emory University

We love this quote from Mark Butt, who for years has shared insightful perspectives on the importance of letters of recommendation in the college admission process. He emphasizes that these letters are not just a formality but are a critical element in telling a student's story. He believes that recommendations can serve as a bridge between a student's personal and academic lives, offering admission committees a more complete picture of who students are and what they might bring to the college environment.

Telling a student's story should not be one-sided: colleges appreciate and give a lot of credence to teacher and school counselor recommendations. Those that also accept (few require) a personal or peer recommendation value this additional input, too. Stories need to be told from various perspectives, including the adults who can speak to a student's triumphs and challenges. Most colleges require at least a school counselor recommendation, and all selective colleges want one, if not two, teacher recommendations. The role of these recommendations is to give "color" to a student's application and add to the story that's already being told in the student's voice via the essays and section of activities.

The Power of Other Voices

The value of the voices in recommendations is primarily their ability to confirm that the story told by a student's application is true. It may also be an opportunity for the recommender to share an anecdote about the applicant that illustrates their points. Our professional organization as college counselors, the National Association for College Admission Counseling, or NACAC, offers guidance on the formatting of recommendations. It suggests a format for school counselor and teacher recommendations that includes concise bulleted statements. Recommendations should focus on specific attributes, achievements, and behaviors that provide clear and personalized insight into the student.

Picking Recommenders

"Choose wisely!" In picking your recommenders, consider the complete story of your application and what voices are missing from it. Because some schools allow only one counselor and teacher recommendation, you want to be sure you are amplifying the perspectives that are most critical to the messages you want to send through your application.

As you plan your recommendation requests, consider the following points:

- **Keep it recent.** Most colleges want to hear from those who have worked with you in 11th or 12th grade.

- **Keep it relevant.** Look for input from those who have worked with you in the areas that interest you. If you want to study a STEM field (science, technology, engineering, mathematics) and your two teacher recommenders are your English and history teachers, college admission officers may scratch their heads.
- **Don't overwhelm.** Do NOT send so many recommendations that the admission office simply stops reading them. In addition to your counselor's recommendation, two from teachers and one from a personal recommender (if permitted) are plenty.
- **Growth is as good as excellence.** You do not have to get recommendations from teachers whose class you aced. Sometimes teachers who watched you struggle and persevere can write more compelling letters about academic drive and character.
- **Don't be redundant.** You are looking for variety in the voices who support you. Asking two math teachers (or of any one subject) is limiting.
- **Tell them why.** When you ask an individual for a recommendation, share with them the reason why you want *their* support in particular. Was there a project you did in their class that you were proud of or other experience that stands out?

In the following sections, we share advice to recommenders according to type: school counselors, teachers, and peer or personal recommenders. We speak to these recommenders directly as *you*. Students may find in this advice ideas for how to request a recommendation and from whom. Students may also want to ask their recommenders to read the section that applies to them.

School Counselors

A school counselor's recommendation is the glue that helps the applicant's story stick together. By providing a balcony view of all that the student is and has done, you allow admission readers to better understand the student's context, strengths, and interests. As you look to highlight different areas of their background, experiences, potential, and character, consider the following structure:

Opening anecdote

- Sets the tone for the rest of the recommendation, highlighting the student's academic abilities and character traits right from the start.

Academic strengths

- Demonstrates a consistent ability to grasp complex concepts in [name of subject].
- Excels in [name of course or type of coursework], showing a deep understanding of [topic].
- Is known for intellectual curiosity and a passion for [subject/field].

Personal qualities

- Resilient and proactive in overcoming challenges, such as [example].
- Exhibits leadership qualities in [context], such as [club, organization, initiative].
- Is respected by peers and faculty for [traits].

Extracurricular involvement

- Actively participates in [activity], demonstrating commitment and growth.
- Successfully balances academic workload with involvement in [activity/organization].

- Plays a crucial role in [project or team], contributing significantly to [outcome].

Conclusion

- Strongly recommend [student's name] for [college/university] due to their [summary of academic/personal strengths].
- Am confident that [student's name] will excel in [field/major] due to their [qualities/experiences].

Sample Recommendation from a School Counselor

Anecdote

One afternoon last spring, I walked past our school's library and noticed something that perfectly encapsulates who Soraya is at her core. She was seated at a table, her math homework spread out before her, but her attention was focused entirely on the seventh-grader across from her. The younger student was clearly struggling, frustration evident in her furrowed brow and tense posture. Without hesitation, Soraya put her own work aside and leaned in to offer quiet words of encouragement and a clear, patient explanation of the math concept. It was a simple, yet profound moment that spoke volumes about Soraya's character: she is someone who not only excels academically but also goes out of her way to lift others up, offering grace and guidance where it is most needed.

Academic Strengths

- *Demonstrates an exceptional aptitude for engineering concepts, consistently excelling in advanced STEM courses such as AP Physics and Calculus.*
- *Applies theoretical knowledge to practical problems, often developing innovative solutions in her engineering projects.*

- *Shows a deep interest in the intersection of technology and societal impact, frequently engaging in independent research on sustainable engineering practices.*

Personal Qualities

- *Soraya is intellectually curious and constantly seeks to deepen her understanding of engineering, often going beyond the curriculum to explore new technologies and methodologies.*
- *Exhibits remarkable perseverance and creativity, especially when faced with challenging projects or concepts that require out-of-the-box thinking.*
- *Highly regarded by both peers and faculty for her ability to approach complex problems with a calm, analytical mindset and a collaborative spirit.*

Extracurricular Involvement

- *Active member and leader of the school's Robotics Club, where she played a pivotal role in designing and building robots for regional competitions, leading her team to victory.*
- *Engaged in several engineering-related internships, where she demonstrated her ability to apply classroom knowledge to real-world challenges, such as optimizing manufacturing processes and developing prototypes.*
- *Regularly volunteers to tutor younger students in math and science, sharing her passion for engineering and inspiring others to pursue careers in STEM fields.*

Conclusion

- *I strongly recommend Soraya for admission to your engineering program. Her academic prowess, coupled with her deep intellectual curiosity and commitment to using engineering to solve real-world problems, makes her an outstanding candidate.*

- *I am confident that Soraya will thrive in your rigorous environment and contribute significantly to your academic community, bringing both her technical skills and her innovative mindset to any challenge she encounters.*

This format emphasizes Soraya's strengths in both academic and extracurricular settings, painting a comprehensive picture of her as a student who is not only passionate about engineering but also dedicated to intellectual growth and helping others.

Teachers

Students have their own ideas about who they are and what they're becoming, but educators have seen them in action in the classroom. We urge teachers to listen to students' stories and then share what's appropriate with colleges to support their potential as learners and contributors to the academic experience in college.

How can this be done effectively? First of all, if you are asked to write a recommendation for a student, please do not ask them for a résumé. If you ask the student for anything, ask them to articulate why they requested a letter from you in particular and if there are any projects, papers, or moments in your class that they hope you will highlight. A teacher's recommendation needs to address how the student did in your class: how they performed in coursework and engaged in class discussion and, ideally, how they supported their classmates. Teachers too often repeat information that school counselors include in their letters of recommendation.

It is the school counselor's job to summarize the experience of students at their school. It is the teacher's job to summarize students' experience in the classroom. The counselor recommendation includes character, activities, leadership, and role in the community. If you have special stories from outside the classroom or other nonacademic thoughts you think should be brought to light, please send them to the counselor. The teacher recommendation is meant to shine a light on the student's intellect, potential, and depth in the classroom setting. Admission officers want to know what sets the student apart as a learner and intellectual risk taker. They do read these letters with care and often have professors on their admission committee who are especially interested in your insight. Here's what should be included:

- Intellectual curiosity
- Role in classroom and group work
- Mastery of material
- If/how they pursued subject knowledge beyond the classroom
- Exemplary projects that highlight their learning

Consider structuring your letter as follows:

Classroom performance

- Consistently performed at the top of the class in [name of subject].
- Demonstrates critical thinking and analytical skills through [type of assignment/project].
- Engages in class discussions, often leading peers with insightful contributions on [topic].

Work ethic and attitude

- Known for a strong work ethic; always prepared and willing to go the extra mile.
- Maintains a positive attitude, even when faced with challenging material.
- Works collaboratively with peers, often assisting others in understanding difficult concepts.

Conclusion about character and integrity

- Exhibits a high level of integrity in both academic and personal interactions.
- Is reliable and trustworthy, often chosen for leadership roles in group assignments.
- Demonstrates empathy and respect for classmates, fostering a supportive learning environment.
- Strongly endorse [student's name] for [college/program] and am confident in their ability to contribute positively to the academic community.

This format helps ensure that the recommendation is clear, focused, and aligned with what colleges are looking for in applicants. Each bullet should provide a snapshot of the student's abilities and character.

Sample Recommendation from a Teacher

Classroom Performance

- *Although Soraya's strengths clearly lie in the sciences, she approached AP American History with the same dedication and intellectual curiosity that defines her work in STEM. Despite the subject being outside her comfort zone, she consistently participated in class discussions, bringing a unique analytical perspective that enriched our conversations about historical events.*
- *Soraya's essays, while not always flawless, showed a remarkable effort to understand and synthesize complex historical themes. Her final paper on the technological impacts of the Industrial Revolution was particularly impressive, showcasing her ability to bridge her passion for engineering with historical analysis.*

Work Ethic and Attitude

- *Soraya is the kind of student every teacher admires: diligent, disciplined, and never one to shy away from a challenge. Even though history was not her strongest subject, she put in countless hours of study and preparation, seeking extra help when needed and always striving to improve.*
- *Her resilience was evident in her willingness to tackle difficult material, even when the grade didn't come easily. Soraya approached every assignment with the intent to learn, rather than just to earn a grade, a quality that speaks volumes about her character.*

Conclusion About Character and Integrity

- *Soraya is a student of exceptional integrity and character. She consistently demonstrated honesty, responsibility, and a deep respect for both her peers and her teachers. Whether collaborating on group projects or working independently, she maintained a high standard of academic ethics.*
- *Her positive attitude and unwavering commitment to doing her best, even in a subject where she faced challenges, are testaments to her maturity and strong moral compass. Soraya is the kind of student who makes a classroom better simply by being in it.*
- *It is my honor to recommend Soraya for admission to your program. Soraya may have earned a B– in my class, but the grade does not fully capture her determination, growth, and the thoughtful approach she brought to her studies. I have no doubt that these qualities, combined with her engineering skills, will make her a standout student in your academic community.*

This recommendation highlights Soraya's strengths, even in a subject that was challenging for her, while also emphasizing her character and work ethic. It provides a well-rounded view of Soraya as a student who is dedicated, intellectually curious, and capable of bridging different disciplines.

Peer and Personal Recommenders

Personal recommendations can come in all shapes and sizes. Some colleges do not allow additional letters beyond a counselor or teacher; others encourage a wide range of perspectives. Only a small handful of colleges and universities require (or "strongly encourage") peer recommendations. Others, however, are open to them if the recommender provides a compelling reason for it. Let's unpack that last part before moving on.

Any additional recommendation needs to add new information or context to an applicant's story. Admission officers have enough to read without being saddled with additional redundant letters. If there is a coach, pastor, mentor, advisor, employer, or other individual who knows the applicant well and can speak to a different part of their story, then, by all means, that person can write a brief letter on the applicant's behalf.

If you have been asked by an applicant to write a peer or personal recommendation, consider the following:

- **Start with context.** How do you know the student and for how long? In what ways did you interact with them, and what is your role in their lives? You don't need to give your entire résumé; one or two sentences about who you are and why you are writing sets the stage for what you will share.
- **Keep it brief.** Your letter should be one page at most. Say what you need to say, and no more.
- **Keep it concrete.** Be specific, using anecdotes and examples of the student's character and commitment. What have you observed about the student's relationships with others, creativity, and engagement in the world around them.

- **Make comparisons.** When appropriate, explain how this student is different from their peers or other young people you have worked with.
- **Proofread.** While neither you nor the student is judged on your writing ability, be sure the letter is free of grammatical errors and typos, as they can distract from the message you are trying to send. Also, make sure you spell the applicant's name correctly throughout.

Sample of a Peer Recommendation (with prompts taken from the form provided by Davidson College)

How long and how well have you known the applicant? Please give information about opportunities you have had to work with or observe the applicant.

I have known Soraya since kindergarten, and 13 years later, she has become a positive influence in school and a thoughtful, generous, and supportive friend. Soraya is truly the most genuine person I know, and I am grateful to call her part of my family as she has made me part of hers. I have been lucky enough to participate in Tylis family pickleball tournaments, fantasy leagues, and family gatherings and to see the respect that this family has for one another. Soraya extends this same kindness, respect, and compassion to her community.

Soraya and I were on the same team for Turning Green's Project Green Challenge (PGC), and I was able to see how Soraya's passion for sustainability flourished into her researched news articles, letters to representatives, and educational infographics that informed the community. We even collaborated on a song pertaining to climate action where Soraya's creative light was able to shine through in an inspiring way. I admire how Soraya would consistently tackle the most difficult of "greenest" daily challenges with a positive attitude, an intellectually curious mindset, and a hunger to make a sustainable change.

What do you see as the applicant's strengths? Please give examples when possible.

Soraya constantly exemplifies the characteristics of a leader who is able to unite members of the community by cultivating a joyful and productive atmosphere. Soraya's optimism is contagious, while her ability to think critically and solve problems creatively stimulates effective solutions to complex challenges. She always establishes a collaborative environment that provides the space for innovative ideas and community involvement to prosper, which I have been able to experience through working with Soraya as co-heads of Earth Committee and as co-facilitators of the Sustainability Council.

She utilized her leadership and experience through these two groups to inspire the project for the PGC finals, which resulted in multiple members from these communities helping with the school's first-ever thrift sale that generated awareness on the issue of fast fashion and raised money for future sustainability initiatives. Soraya was a crucial part of engaging parents, faculty members, and students from various grade levels to donate clothes, assist in preparing the donations, raise awareness through newsletters, posters, and talking to others, set up an abundance of items, and help run the final event. Soraya's ability to utilize her communication skills and community understanding produced a legacy of giving back through annual thrift sales and displayed her altruistic nature.

What do you consider to be the applicant's weaknesses? Again, it would be helpful to give specific examples by referring to activities or projects in which a weakness has emerged.

I would like to see Soraya leverage her expertise and passion to mentor rising students to become collaborative leaders in the academic setting. She can learn to be more vocal in this sense so that her work ethic and cheerful energy can influence others. She has a unique set of talents and the ability to rally people toward a common goal that could help shape the next generation of leaders.

Soraya has demonstrated this skill set as she mentors an ensemble in her choir. Yet she can build on this foundation and relate her mentorship experience to our school community even more so.

Do Recommendations Matter?

Yes, recommendations matter. We want to encourage teachers, counselors, and anyone else writing on a student's behalf to take this request seriously. Often, admission officers will use letters of recommendation to validate what the student says about themselves or to gain a different perspective for evaluating who they will be as a college student. Recommendation letters matter a lot for character references. Students can have excellent grades and study hard, but are they good people? Will they contribute to a college or university's classrooms and community culture? Will they be someone admission officers can see going deeper into academic disciplines and being a productive college student? These questions are not easy to answer for a 17- or 18-year-old. Still, in a letter of recommendation, the recommender must do their best to support the student's story and ambition and speak adult-to-adult to the admission officer about the student's candidacy.

CHAPTER 12

Harnessing Artificial Intelligence

Admission readers are quick to tell students, "We just want to hear your voice." The truth is that as a college applicant, it's very hard to know exactly what that is. Utilizing AI tools is an opportunity for students to react to a format, style, or word choice that is not uniquely theirs and then work with it. I think about it like still-wet clay that has form but needs detail and allows the writer-sculptor to add detail, specificity, and color. Ultimately, that is "voice," and that's what colleges are solving for by asking students to write in the first place.

—Rick Clark, Executive Director of
Enrollment Management, Georgia Tech

If you are not using artificial intelligence daily, you're missing an opportunity to simplify your life. The future is now, and we have hope and curiosity for AI rather than fear and frustration. While we understand why some of our educational colleagues criticize AI as the demise of human thinking, creativity, art, and especially writing, we also think about possibilities and opportunities.

In the 1970s, my (Shereem's) mother gifted me a T-shirt with the United Negro College Fund's slogan on the front, "A mind is a terrible thing to waste," and I wore it proudly. That slogan has stuck with me for the past 50 years because I knows that we, as human beings, will not be wasting our minds just because of innovation.

AI synthesizes information. It allows us to ask it to combine disparate bits of information, art, and intelligence to form something distinctive of our creation. What we must not do is allow it to take over our innate human intelligence.

As AI pertains to college essay writing, the complexities and scruples that arise are glaring. The issue of originality looms large. If students rely too heavily on AI to craft their essays, they risk entering a gray area of authorship where it becomes difficult to discern who truly wrote the essay. The most pressing issue is the risk of AI eroding the authenticity of a student's voice.

We hope by now that you understand the college essay is, at its heart, a personal narrative. It is a space where students can reflect on their experiences, articulate their values, and express who they are beyond grades and test scores. When students let AI generate or significantly alter essay content, there's a danger that the student's authentic voice will get lost in the process. The essay could become less a reflection of the student and more a product of algorithmic suggestions—polished but impersonal.

This chapter is intentionally brief because, by the time this book is released, AI will be even more proficient than it is today. As succinctly as possible, we aim to cut through the noise, offering ethical options for how AI can democratize the college application process. It has the potential to level the playing field, offering personalized support that might otherwise be unavailable to many students, and we support that.

How can students preserve the integrity of the college essay as a genuine reflection of their experiences and character in an age where AI is increasingly capable of mimicking human expression? This is not just a technological issue but also a philosophical one.

The ethical use of AI begins with leveraging its strengths—such as generating organization frameworks, suggesting thematic connections, and prompting reflective questions. Its role can be likened to that of a highly efficient research assistant, which helps to manage the often-overwhelming demands of brainstorming and structuring an essay, thereby allowing the student to focus more deeply on the substance of their narrative. This approach respects the integrity of voice, not diminishing it but amplifying it. Might AI become a crutch? Maybe, but it's not for us to judge. We would rather offer a few suggestions on how it can be used, in our opinion, ethically and effectively.

Expanding the Horizon of Ideas

AI can help students broaden their brainstorming by suggesting themes, topics, or angles they might not have initially considered. For instance, AI can analyze the prompts provided by colleges and generate a list of potential topics based on keywords. This can be valuable for students who struggle to identify experiences or aspects of their lives worth exploring in an essay.

Helping to Organize Thoughts

Once a student has a general idea of what they want to write about, AI can assist in organizing their generated thoughts into a coherent structure. It can suggest ways to outline the essay, offering frameworks that help the student visualize how their story might unfold. For example, AI can propose different organizational patterns—such as a chronological, thematic, or problem-solution structure—that might fit the student's narrative. This support can be crucial for students struggling to translate a jumble of ideas into a clear, logical progression. The critical ethical consideration here is that the student should retain control over how their essay is ultimately structured, ensuring that the final product reflects their voice and intent.

Identifying Grammatical Errors and Typos

For years, we have been big fans of Grammarly. It's an AI-powered digital writing assistant that helps users improve their writing by identifying and suggesting corrections for grammatical errors, spelling mistakes, punctuation issues, and stylistic inconsistencies. This, and other AI tools, can be incredibly useful for catching grammatical errors, typos, and basic sentence structure problems that might slip through student's and parent's proofreading.

Providing Feedback

Not every student has a team of supporters ready and willing to read their essays and offer insight. AI can be an effective means of leveling the playing field in admission when applicants seek feedback. Imagine, for example, that once a student has a strong draft of a personal statement or supplemental essay, they feed it to an AI chatbot and ask it to respond with what it learned about them through their writing. Perhaps the student could instruct the AI chatbot to list three themes, values, or strengths that the essay highlighted. Armed with this response, the student can reflect on whether the message they hoped to convey was received.

Follow the Rules

The ways that colleges and universities are approaching AI vary greatly. The same holds true for their admission offices. Some schools encourage applicants to use AI as a tool in ethical ways, and others have draconian policies that warn against its use. At the time of this writing, many colleges have not released any policy or statement at all about AI, trusting that students will use their judgment for what is appropriate use and authentic results. Make sure that you understand any policy that a college may have, and do not be afraid to ask what the college's perspective on AI is when you attend a recruiting program or visit campus. Simply stated, if a college has rules about using AI in applying for admission, follow them. If not, take advantage of AI in the measured ways we have suggested.

We want to end this brief survey by repeating our earlier qualification: the AI tools available at the time we wrote this chapter will be updated or outdated by the time you read it. Rather than viewing AI as an adversary to authenticity in the college application, we should learn how to make it an ally that can help to democratize access to higher education for diverse students.

Conclusion

Is It Done?

Our stories are never done. Students often ask whether their personal statement and other college admission writing is "done" or "good enough." We can always do more and be more, but at a certain point, we need to put a stake in the ground and say enough is enough. Be confident that the work you have done reflects your experiences and character. If you have followed the guidance in this book, you will have set yourself up for success.

Our stories don't always need to have a happy ending, nor do they need to be wrapped up with a bow or some kind of significant lesson learned. These are college essays, not parables. Writing about yourself takes courage and patience. We hope what you've taken away from this book is a deep understanding that your voice matters. In the end, college admission officers simply want to learn more about you as an individual and what makes you tick. Writing is just one part of your application, but it is one in which you can shine in unique ways. Seize these opportunities and put in the time and effort to lift up what makes you, you. Once you have done that, let go. You could always change a word here or there or perhaps remedy a misplaced comma. Do your best, but don't obsess.

Our hope is that you will seize the opportunity to apply to college and grow as a writer and communicator. This can be a learning experience and a fitting culmination to the skills you have been acquiring in high school. We also hope you will be intentional about your self-reflection and use the application not just to get into college but also to deepen your relationships with others and to build character.

Good luck!

To Parents: The Approach to Writing Starts at Home

We have both supported a daughter and a son through the college application experience. Each of these four young people approached writing their essays and their interactions with us as fathers differently. As admission professionals, we are immersed in college counseling daily, and this allows us a unique perspective and an appreciation for seizing these opportunities to learn and grow with our children. We close with short summaries of how our children's application writing went for us. We hope these will reassure you and encourage you to take advantage of this experience as a family.

Brennan

I chose to be super hands-off throughout the college admission process to the extent that both children had to ask me to be more deliberate with feedback. My son wrote his personal statement at the start of the summer before senior year and only in the final stages did he ask me for input on the flow of his essay. As I related in chapter 3, he wrote about his relationship with his grandfather and the role of storytelling in our family. He used this topic to highlight how he uses art and music to tell stories.

My daughter spent her entire summer away as a camp counselor and debated possible topics throughout the fall of her senior year. She wanted my involvement from the get-go with brainstorming and sought my personal and professional assessment of potential topics. She is a verbal processor, and our most meaningful conversations are during evening walks. As feet move, ideas flow, and I appreciated the opportunity to be a sounding board. A recruited athlete, she knew her accomplishments and dedication as a rower would shine through other parts of the application, so she wanted to focus her essay on other experiences that had been impactful. In the end she wrote about her emerging leadership in school life and how one does not have to be the best at something to lead.

Both of my children worked through a series of drafts but didn't obsess. They told their stories as best they could but also acknowledged that, as young adults, their stories are evolving. In the end, they were accepted to colleges they were excited to attend and are enjoying successful experiences there.

Shereem

I had no reservations when it came to helping my oldest daughter and son with their college essays. My daughter, Sydney, wrote about her experience at the University of Southern California for a summer program and how it opened her eyes to opportunity. Being from Harlem, New York, and not having traveled extensively, she saw a life outside her bubble. Excited and intrigued, she learned to take chances and realized that as she approached high school graduation, her life was and still is all about choices. The newfound confidence that fueled her essay led her to choose Xavier University in Louisiana, where she majored in education and had her early professional career as a teacher. I am so proud of her.

My son, a student-athlete, traveled a much different path, and we have had to adjust to a changing college athletic landscape post-COVID. However, I have fond memories of our time together in the car, brainstorming extensively. Yes, there were times that we disagreed on what he should write about, but eventually he saw his essay as an opportunity to write about his influence on his twin sisters. Eight years older than them, he remembered being an only child and how their lives changed him forever, including seeing himself in each of them in distinct ways. The core of the essay, written three years ago, remains the same: sharing your life with someone and recognizing your humanity—flaws and all—in others is awesome.

So many college essays are about challenges and triumphs, and that's fine, but there's something about stepping out of your comfort zone and writing about a subject that no one ever expects you to. It was refreshing for my son to share something about himself that was truly personal, vulnerable, and revealing.

There you have it. That is our story, and we are sticking to it. In the months since we started writing this book, we have both turned 50, lost loved ones, parented tweens, teens, and twenty-somethings, started new professional initiatives, grown personally, traveled with our families, faced challenges, and celebrated successes. Our lives and perspectives constantly evolve as the world around us changes rapidly. Artificial intelligence alone has impacted our daily work in ways we never anticipated a year ago.

The years ahead will bring even more milestones as our children graduate college and launch into careers. Our friendship and collaboration have deepened, and our personal and professional narratives have developed. We are, at heart, storytellers who are inspired by our work with young people to articulate their own backgrounds, interests, strengths, and unique qualities and values.

ACKNOWLEDGMENTS

Joint

Thank you to the Westtown community, where our shared story began. We are grateful to our college counselor and professional mentor, Susan Tree, for launching our careers. Thank you to our coauthors Rick Clark and Timothy Fields for your support and collaboration. Finally, to our editor and friend Greg Britton and to Hopkins Press, your belief in our stories and years of support have allowed us to share our message widely. Thank you.

Brennan

To my father, Timothy, one of the finest storytellers there is. Your love and support cannot be captured in words. I am eternally grateful for all you do for our family and world. To my children, Sam and Becca, I am immensely proud of the adults you have become and the life stories you are creating.

To my brothers, Daron and Justin, your loving support and guidance lifts me up. To my sisters-in-law, KC and Jessa; my nieces and nephews, Charlie, Malcolm, Phoebe, and Skyler; and to Meredy and family, you brighten our lives and make our family full.

To the many educators who have taught and mentored me, you have given me the tools and space to write my story and let my life speak. To all the colleagues and institutions who have contributed immeasurably to my growth, professionally and personally.

To the friends I have lost, especially Dennis Gainty and Matthew Struckmeyer, your memory is central to how I live my life, and you each made me a better writer and human.

To my circle of friends, near and far, you know who you are and how much you mean to me.

Shereem

I am fortunate to have family, friends, and fraternity.

To my TeamHB: I hope my model inspires you to dream and work.

To those who I can call and who can call me anytime and anywhere, thank you. To Auntie Irene, Tia Lerna, Gail Karpf, and Dianne Garrett, so much of my story is because of your influence. Thank you.

To Tim Fields: thank you for always reminding me to be about the people.

To the men of Omega Psi Phi Fraternity Inc., thank you for loving and inspiring me. I am honored to be a part of our legacy.

APPENDIX

Practice Writing Prompts

Use the following writing prompts as a tool to brainstorm. Do not set out to write a college essay and do not overthink what you are writing. Keep the stakes low and relieve yourself of pressure. Set a timer for 20 minutes and just start freewriting in reaction to a prompt. Try not to stop writing during that time even if you change direction in what you are putting down. Take a break between prompts or try one on different days.

My proudest moment was . . .

A victory I had was . . .

My most shameful moment was . . .

My most embarrassing moment was . . .

My best birthday was . . .

The person I admire most is . . .

My favorite story about a sibling is when . . .

The person who taught me the most is . . .

An adventure I had was . . .

My number one dream for the future is . . .

If I could do anything right now, I would . . .

If I could be with anyone right now, it would be . . .

The most difficult time of my life was . . .

Brainstorming Questions

Question: What are the most significant experiences that have shaped who you are today?

Exercise: Spend 10 minutes freewriting about a pivotal moment in your life. This could be a challenge you overcame, a major achievement, or a defining experience that has deeply impacted you. Don't worry about grammar or structure; just get your thoughts down on paper or screen.

Question: What values and beliefs are most important to you, and how have they influenced your decisions and actions?

Exercise: Create a list of your core values and beliefs. Then think of examples where these values have guided your actions, decisions, and interactions with others. This exercise can help you identify themes for your personal statement. Here are 20 examples of values to consider:

1. **Resilience** demonstrates your ability to overcome challenges and bounce back from setbacks.
2. **Integrity** illustrates your honesty, ethics, and strong moral principles.
3. **Empathy** shows your understanding and compassion toward others' experiences and perspectives.
4. **Perseverance** highlights your determination and persistence in the face of obstacles.
5. **Curiosity** exhibits your strong desire to learn and explore new ideas and experiences.
6. **Leadership** showcases your ability to guide, inspire, and influence others positively.
7. **Responsibility** demonstrates your accountability for your actions and commitments.

8. **Creativity** highlights your ability to think outside the box and approach problems with innovative solutions.
9. **Diversity and inclusion** promotes an appreciation of differences, an advocacy of fairness, and a feeling of belonging.
10. **Service** shows commitment to helping others and contributing to your community.
11. **Adaptability** demonstrates flexibility and the ability to adjust to new events and environments.
12. **Teamwork** emphasizes your ability to work collaboratively with others toward a common goal.
13. **Independence** showcases your ability to take initiative and work autonomously.
14. **Respect** demonstrates that you honor yourself, others, and differing opinions.
15. **Passion** highlights your enthusiasm and dedication to an interest or cause.
16. **Humility** shows a willingness to learn from others and acknowledge your limitations.
17. **Courage** demonstrates your ability to face fears and take risks for growth and improvement.
18. **Innovation** emphasizes your ability to bring new ideas and improvements to existing processes or situations.
19. **Gratitude** shows appreciation for the opportunities and support you have received.
20. **Self-discipline** highlights your ability to stay focused, organized, and committed to your goals.

Question: Who are the people that have had the greatest influence on your life, and what have you learned from them?

Exercise: Make a list of the people who have significantly impacted your life. Next to each name, write a few sentences about what you've learned from them and how they've influenced your personal growth. This can help you identify meaningful relationships and mentorship you might want to include in your personal statement or supplemental essays.

Question: What challenges have you faced, and how have you overcome them?

Exercise: Reflect on a major obstacle you've encountered and write a short narrative about how you dealt with it. Focus on the steps you took, the skills you developed, and the lessons you learned. This exercise will help you frame your experiences in a way that showcases your resilience and problem-solving abilities.

Question: What are your goals for the future, and how have your past experiences prepared you to achieve them?

Exercise: Write a letter to your future self, describing your goals and aspirations for the next 5–10 years. Include how your past experiences have prepared you for these goals and what steps you plan to take to achieve them. This exercise can help you connect your past experiences with your future aspirations in your application.

What Not to Include in a College Essay

Your college essay is an opportunity to showcase your personality, experiences, and goals to an admission committee. While it's important to be authentic and personal, there are certain topics that should be avoided. This list lets you know what not to write about to ensure your application remains appropriate, respectful, and professional.

Romantic relationships. Discussing romantic relationships can be too personal and might make the reader uncomfortable. These stories can overshadow important aspects of your character and experiences. Avoid writing about your significant other or getting into details of your romantic life. Instead, focus on personal growth and achievements that don't involve your romantic relationships.

Sex. This topic is highly personal and can be inappropriate for a college essay. It may also lead to discomfort for the reader and can detract from the professionalism of your application. Refrain from mentioning any experiences or opinions related to sex. Keep the content respectful and suitable for a broad audience.

Drug use. Mentioning drug use, even if it's in the past, can raise concerns about your judgment and character. It's best to avoid this topic entirely.

Alcohol. Similar to drug use, discussing alcohol consumption can create a negative impression, particularly if you are under 21 years old. It can also be seen as promoting unhealthy behavior.

Inappropriate or offensive humor. What might seem funny to you could be offensive or inappropriate to someone else, especially an admission officer. Humor can be tricky to convey in writing and can easily be misinterpreted.

INDEX